THE QUESTION OF LANGUAGE IN HEIDEGGER'S HISTORY OF BEING

Contemporary Studies in Philosophy and the Human Sciences

Series editor: John Sallis
Associate editors: Hugh J. Silverman and David Farrell Krell

Published

* Robert Bernasconi: **The Question of Language in Heidegger's History of Being**
  Peter Caws: **Structuralism**
  Mikel Dufrenne: **In the Presence of the Sensuous**
* John Llewelyn: **Beyond Metaphysics?**
  Louis Marin: **Utopics: Spatial Play**
* Graeme Nicholson: **Seeing and Reading**
* Otto Pöggeler: **Martin Heidegger's Path of Thinking**
* Charles E. Scott: **The Language of Difference**
  Jacques Taminiaux: **Dialectic and Difference**
  David Wood: **The Deconstruction of Time**

Forthcoming

James W. Bernauer: **Michel Foucault's Force of Flight**
David Farrell Krell: **On the Verge**

* Also available in paperback

THE QUESTION OF LANGUAGE IN HEIDEGGER'S HISTORY OF BEING

by

ROBERT BERNASCONI

Humanities Press International, Inc.
Atlantic Highlands, NJ

First published in 1985. Reprinted in paperback 1989 by
HUMANITIES PRESS INTERNATIONAL, INC.,
Atlantic Highlands, NJ 07716.

Library of Congress Cataloging-in-Publication Data

Bernasconi, Robert.
  The question of language in Heidegger's history of
being.

  (Contemporary studies in philosophy and the human
sciences)
  Bibliography: p.
  Includes index.
  1. Heidegger, Martin, 1889-1976.   I. Title.
II. Series.
B3279.H49B454   1984   193   84-3739
ISBN 0-391-03093-0
ISBN 0-391-03617-3 (Pbk.)

Printed in the United States of America

To my father
—and in memory of my mother

Words strain,
Crack and sometimes break, under the burden,
Under the tension, slip, slide, perish,
Decay with imprecision, will not stay in place,
Will not stay still.

T. S. Eliot, "Burnt Norton"

Contents

Preface   ix

Abbreviations   xi

I   The Dialogue with the Previous History of Thinking:
     Hegel and Heidegger

     1. Truth and Refutation in the History of Philosophy   1
     2. The End of Philosophy — and Its Beginning   5
     3. Remembrance in Hegel and Heidegger   9
        Notes   12

II   *Aletheia* and the Concealment of Concealing

     1. Truth and Unconcealment   15
     2. An Ambiguity in Plato   17
     3. Heidegger's Rereading of his Essay on Plato   23
        Notes   26

III "History is Seldom": Hölderlin and Heidegger

     1. The Dialogue between Poet and Thinker   29
     2. The Work of Art and the Naming of the Holy   35
     3. The Default of God and Another Beginning   41
        Notes   46

IV   "Where the word is wanting...": George and Heidegger

     1. George's Poem *Das Wort*: Two Views of Language   49
     2. The Thinker's Experience and the Question of Metaphysics 54
     3. Renunciation and the Transformation of *Logos*   58
        Notes   63

V   The Saying of a Turning: Heidegger and Technology

    1. The Essence of Truth and the Truth of Essence   65
    2. Technology and the Break with Essence as Permanent Enduring   69
    3. The Saying of a Turning and the Speculative Proposition   76
    Notes   78

VI   *Ereignis*: Experience and Remembrance

    1. Experience: *Erlebnis* and *Erfahrung*   81
    2. *Ereignis* and the Overcoming of Metaphysics   86
    3. *Ereignis* and the Transformation of Language   90
    Notes   95

Bibliography   99

Index   107

Preface

The present study is not an attempt to render an account of Heidegger's history of Being; that history is not a story and cannot be retold as one. This book is concerned with the insight that introduces us to the history of Being and the transformation in our relation to language that accompanies that insight.

I have proceeded, for the most part, by a series of readings of Heideggerian texts. No attempt has been made to cover the whole of the Heideggerian *corpus*: these are only incisions into the *corpus* and the interpretation offered is only provisional, though not particularly on grounds of incompleteness, but in the sense indicated in the final chapter.

In addition to Heidegger himself, two other thinkers dominate this book: Hegel and Derrida. Much may be found in what follows about the relation between Hegel and Heidegger, although, of course, there remains a great deal more to be said. But I have mentioned Derrida in only a few references. In particular I would ask anyone who would wish to label my efforts a "Derridian reading" to consult a companion essay to this book, "The Transformation of Language at Another Beginning" in *Research in Phenomenology* volume 13, 1983. My sense of the proper response that should be made to Heidegger as read here, and indeed to Derrida, is barely indicated, both in the present book and in that article. I hope that it may one day be presented in a series of essays on which I am working that take their starting point in Levinas.

I have tried whenever possible to supply references to available translations as well as to the originals. The reader should be aware that I have adopted the convention of altering translations for the sake of uniformity or accuracy, without signaling the change.

I would like to thank the following, all of whom read an earlier draft of the following work and were generous in offering their comments and advice: Walter Brogan, Tina Chanter, Rickie Damman, Parvis Emad, Michel Haar, David Krell, John Sallis, Jacques Taminiaux, and Anthony Thorlby.

Abbreviations

BW   *Basic Writings*. Edited by D. F. Krell. New York: Harper & Row, 1977, and London: Routledge & Kegan Paul, 1978.

EB   *Existence and Being*. Translated by R. Hull and A. Crick. London: Vision, 1949.

ED   *Erläuterungen zu Hölderlins Dichtung*. Frankfurt: Klostermann. Pages 1-143, zweite Auflage, 1951. Pages 152-193, vierte Auflage, 1971: page numbers of second edition in margin.

EGT   *Early Greek Thinking*. Translated by D. F. Krell and F. A. Capuzzi. New York: Harper & Row, 1975.

EM   *Einführung in die Metaphysik*. Tübingen: Niemeyer, 1966. Translated by R. Manheim as *An Introduction to Metaphysics*. New Haven: Yale University Press, 1973.

EP   *The End of Philosophy*. Translated by J. Stambaugh. New York: Harper & Row, 1973, and London: Souvenir, 1975.

GP   *Vorlesungen über die Geschichte der Philosophie*. 3 Bände. Frankfurt: Suhrkamp, 1971. Translated by E. S. Haldane as *Hegel's Lectures on the History of Philosophy*. 3 vols. London: Routledge & Kegan Paul, and New York: Humanities, 1968.

H   *Holzwege*. Frankfurt: Klostermann, 1972.

HCE   *Hegel's Concept of Experience*. New York: Harper & Row, 1970.

ID   *Identität und Differenz*. Pfullingen: Neske, 1957. Translated by J. Stambaugh as *Identity and Difference*. New York: Harper & Row, 1969.

NI   *Nietzsche*, Band 1, Pfullingen: Neske, 1961.

NII   *Nietzsche*, Band 2. Pfullingen: Neske, 1961.

Ni   *Nietzsche*, vol. 1. The Will to Power as Art. Translated by D. F. Krell. New York: Harper & Row, and London: Routledge & Kegan Paul, 1979.

P   Plato's Doctrine of Truth. Translated by J. Barlow. In *Philosophy in the Twentieth Century*, edited by W. Barrett and H. D. Aiken, vol. 3. New York: Harper & Row, 1971.

PLT   *Poetry, Language, Thought.* Translated by A. Hofstadter. New York: Harper & Row, 1971.

PS   *Phänomenologie des Geistes*, Gesammelte Werke Band 9. Hrsg. W. Bonsiepen und R. Heede. Hamburg: Meiner, 1980. Translated by A. V. Miller as *Phenomenology of Spirit.* Oxford: Oxford University Press, 1978.

QT   *The Question concerning Technology and Other Essays.* Translated by W. Lovitt. New York: Harper & Row, 1977.

SD   *Zur Sache des Denkens.* Tübingen: Niemeyer, 1969.

SZ   *Sein und Zeit.* Tübingen: Niemeyer, 1967. Translated by J. Macquarrie and J. Robinson as *Being and Time.* Oxford: Basil Blackwell, 1962.

TB   *On Time and Being.* Translated by J. Stambaugh. New York: Harper & Row, 1977.

TK   *Die Technik und die Kehre.* Pfullingen: Neske, 1962.

UK   *Der Ursprung des Kunstwerkes.* Stuttgart: Reclam, 1960.

US   *Unterwegs zur Sprache.* Pfullingen: Neske, 1959.

VA   *Vorträge und Aufsätze.* Pfullingen: Neske, 1954.

VS   *Vier Seminare.* Frankfurt: Klostermann, 1977.

W   *Wegmarken.* Frankfurt: Klostermann, 1967.

WB   "The Way Back into the Ground of Metaphysics." Translated by W. Kaufmann. In *Existentialism from Dostoevsky to Sartre.* New York: Meridian, 1956.

WD   *Was heisst Denken?* Tübingen: Niemeyer, 1954. Translated by F. D. Wieck and J. Glenn Gray as *What Is Called Thinking?* New York: Harper & Row, 1968.

WL   *On the Way to Language.* Translated by P. Hertz and J. Stambaugh. New York: Harper & Row, 1971.

THE QUESTION OF LANGUAGE IN HEIDEGGER'S HISTORY OF BEING

Chapter One
The Dialogue with the Previous History of Thinking: Hegel and Heidegger

1. Truth and Refutation in the History of Philosophy

Modern continental philosophy is defined by its readiness to face the challenge posed by the recognition of the historicity of philosophy. This is the fundamental issue to which both Hegel and Heidegger address themselves to the point of calling into question the very notion of history. But there has been a tendency, for as long as twenty years or more, for philosophers, particularly in Germany, to exhibit a growing lack of resolution in their approach to this question. This is well illustrated by their attempts to unite the perspectives of Hegel and Heidegger toward history, without due regard for the genuine differences between them. Even though the question of the apparent similarity between Hegel and Heidegger had been repeatedly raised in Heidegger's seminars, his answers did not stem the tide of syncretism.[1]

Gadamer's *Truth and Method* was a major influence in this respect. The book was enthusiastically hailed as presenting a particularly intelligible version of Heidegger's views, without due consideration being given to the question of the extent to which Gadamer had departed from Heidegger in order to accommodate Hegel.[2] Gadamer emphasizes the notion of experience common to both thinkers so as to provide the basis for his own account of our openness to what is said in the tradition. But this simply reflects the fact that his main concern, both in the book and in terms of what was possible for hermeneutics in general as he understood it, was not that of discriminating between different standpoints. Gadamer had taken over from Hegel the notion of the fundamental continuity of all thinking; it was, in consequence, simply not possible for him to entertain the view that there was no such thing as "Heidegger's philosophy" and hence no basis for a juxtaposition of Heidegger and Hegel that had not first addressed the question of where that comparison stood in respect of philosophy — inside or outside, or in some third "place" neither inside nor outside but somehow both and neither. And yet this is, as we shall see, precisely the question that governs Heidegger's own understanding of his relation to previous thinking.

1

Gadamer is content to situate himself as the heir of both Hegel and Heidegger in his understanding of the historicity of philosophy, while at the same time refusing to take from Hegel the reference to absolute knowledge or from Heidegger the reference to Being. Whether any sense can be made of Hegel's concepts without absolute knowing, or of Heidegger's words without the question of Being, was simply not asked, because it was supposed that all such constructions were the product of a form of a priori reasoning that in attempting to understand history had recourse to a framework that set itself above history. Whether that is indeed the case for Heidegger, as it might be said to be for Hegel, will have to be investigated. But for the moment it is worth noticing that some of the best scholars were coming to reflect at least one aspect of Gadamer's position. Gadamer characterizes the task of his philosophical hermeneutics as that of "moving back along the path of Hegel's *Phenomenology of Spirit.*"[3] Meanwhile evidence was being amassed that Heidegger's history of the growing oblivion of Being was itself basically a reversal of Hegel's ladder of ascent to the absolute.[4] If that were the case then there would indeed be grounds for recognizing Gadamer's appropriation of Heidegger as quite legitimate.

That there must be in Heidegger frequent points of contact with Hegel is clear; any rethinking of the history of thinking must take place with reference to Hegel. Prior to Hegel, the dominant model of what constituted a philosophical approach to the history of philosophy had been provided by Aristotle, for whom one would, through an examination of previous positions, come to adopt those that were well stated and be on guard against those which were not.[5] Today it is hard, in the light of what that approach became and the rhetoric that has been employed in its name, to recognize that dictum, which is of itself no more than a demand for openness, as historical at all and not simply an exercise in employing one's arguments and having the views one already holds confirmed. Hegel's stature as the thinker who succeeded in adopting an approach to the history of philosophy that was at once both philosophical and historical means that all attempts to rethink the history of philosophy in its historicity can only take place in a language indebted to him. The primary question that has to be asked is not whether we find such verbal points of contact between Hegel and Heidegger, although the inevitability of such echoes has to be accounted for by any "philosophy" of the history of philosophy. The question to be asked, however, is better indicated by a comment Heidegger himself made in the 1927 lecture series now published as *Basic Problems of Phenomenology.* "Hegel saw everything that is possible. But the question is whether he saw it from the radical centre of philosophy, whether he exhausted all the possibilities of the beginning so as to say that he is at the end."[6]

In the introductory remarks to the *Lectures on the History of Philosophy*, Hegel announced his resolution to overcome such relativism as was arising from the growing awareness of philosophy's long history. Hegel's contribution, which was decisively to transform the practice of philosophy, was to insist that the passage from one philosophy to another was the work, not of timeless criticism, but of time—or, more accurately, of "Spirit emptied out into time" (PG 433; tr. 492). Hegel came to regard the familiar procedures of refutation and counter-argument as extrinsic to philosophy in its proper sense. He himself may on occasion have been critical of his predecessors; there are some notable instances in the *Science of Logic* when, for example, he makes Kant his target. But criticism of one's predecessors is a form of philosophical pettiness, a kind of vanity that arises out of particularity (GP III 461; tr. 553). This partiality is overcome provisionally in the thinker's relation to his time, which is a relation to the universal, and it is overcome ultimately in the unification without eclecticism of the various philosophies of the past in the System of Philosophy.

The System of Philosophy is the proof that these diverse philosophies are parts of a single whole. In respect of mathematical and historical knowledge it is otherwise, but any philosophical proposition that is presented as a fixed result is, on those grounds alone, one-sided and therefore false. No philosophical position can be regarded in isolation from its place within the history of philosophy. "The true is the whole. But the whole is only the essence completing itself through its development" (PG 19; tr. 11). What this means is that the systematic presentation of the truth lies outside the opposition of the assertion of truth and its denial. When we think of Hegel's concept of truth as certitude, and that is how Hegel himself thought of it, we should not neglect the fact that Hegel's speculative-dialectical method departs from the Cartesian method that guarantees truth as certitude in Descartes' sense of the word. Hegel calls the philosophical way with language that departs from the assertion, "speculative". "The true is the whole" is accordingly a speculative proposition. Insofar as he speaks speculatively, Hegel's thinking bequeaths no fixed results. Furthermore, his exposition is dialectical; it is governed by "the progressive development of truth" (PG 10; tr. 2). What is partial is not opposed from outside, but taken up and developed. That development culminates in the sublation *(Aufhebung)* of time itself, which takes place when we recognize ourselves as heirs of the past. Although in attaining the standpoint of the System we have come to occupy a position of superiority over what has gone before, it is not a position from which we can reject the past: it makes us what we are.

Hegel's discovery of the history of philosophy provides the essential background for Heidegger's approach to his predecessors. Like Hegel, he departs from the procedure of critical refutation as the means by which the truth is to be attained in the context of the dialogue with one's predecessors. He addresses himself to the arguments of a philosopher only to clarify what underlies them, not to meet them on their own terms. "All refutation in the field of essential thinking is foolish. Strife among thinkers is the 'lover's quarrel' concerning the thing itself" (W 166-67; BW 215-16). To Heidegger's critics this is evidence of an uncritical approach, but to Heidegger himself it was obvious that one did not turn to the history of philosophy simply to substantiate one's own position.

Heidegger calls Hegel the only Western thinker who has thoughtfully experienced the history of thinking (H 298; EGT 14). To experience that thought has a history is to pass beyond the assumption that thinking is governed by standards that are, even if only in principle, equally accessible to all thinkers. It means to accept that every thinker belongs to his or her time. If we continue to measure past thinkers in terms of their proximity to the truth as a timeless standard, then we submit the relation between thinkers and their times to an inappropriate measure, the consequence of which is relativism. The experience of the history of thinking is only preserved where it gives rise to a transformation of the concept of truth.

The readings of texts from the history of philosophy that Heidegger offered both in his teaching and his published writings were always attempts to hear the "truth" of the text, which resided in a claim made by the text on its reader. This is the point of contact between Heidegger's approach and Gadamerian hermeneutics: truth lay not in what was said explicitly in the text as something directly accessible to antiquarian scholarship, but in the unsaid which emerges only in a questioning dialogue with it. Before he began to withdraw from the word *Being* as the source of many of the misconceptions about his thinking, Heidegger called this truth 'the truth of Being'. Like Hegel, Heidegger no longer applies the traditional concept of truth to the tradition. Truth in Heidegger is understood always in terms of the play (which is no opposition) of concealment and unconcealment, and the phrase "truth of Being" refers to those occasions when Being has been brought to language in one of its historical characters only to remain concealed until it is heard at the end of philosophy. What is heard in the dialogue between thinkers does not belong merely to the past; if it did, there would be no dialogue. In *Being and Time*, Heidegger described it in terms of a "destruction." "By taking *the question of Being as our clue*, we are to *destroy* the traditional content of ancient ontology until we arrive at the primordial experiences in which we achieved our first ways of determining the nature of Being—ways which have guided us ever since" (SZ 22; tr. 44). Whether he is talking of the destruction of the history of ontology, the overcoming of metaphysics, or of leaving metaphysics behind, what is at issue is the changed relation to Being that has now been brought to light as spoken by the thinkers of the tradition.

This was for some time overlooked because of the ambiguity of the word *Being*. One of the major sources of confusion concerning *Being and Time* arises from the way that Heidegger, in the opening pages, gives the impression that he is taking up the same question that Plato and Aristotle asked with the question "What is Being?". Heidegger later acknowledged that what he calls 'Being' and what the philosophers of the tradition called 'Being' are by no means the same.

When metaphysics says 'Being', we should hear instead, according to Heidegger, *Seiende* ('beings') or *Seiendheit* ('beingness'). The confusions that arise from this ambiguity of the word *Being* are not simply mistakes (W 199-200; WB 211). That Heidegger must use a word drawn from the tradition to say more than the tradition could say, and thus in the process finds himself drawn back into that tradition, arises from a necessity that repeats itself in the ambiguity of all language at the time of the gathering of philosophy (US 109; WL 19).

The phrase "the oblivion of Being" provides another example of the difficulties that arise from Heidegger's language of Being. The insight into the history of Being seems to be the negation of the oblivion of Being. But what virtually all Heidegger's writings explore is how the experience of the oblivion of Being is an experience of the historical nature of philosophy that reveals what is said in the unsaid of that history. This book is concerned with the way the thinker of the time of technology lacks a word for Being and yet thereby discovers that naming Being has been the previously unrecognized task of the philosopher. The experience of the oblivion of Being is the experience of the end of philosophy because the thinker discovers thoughtfully that he or she can no longer do what the philosopher did. But the end of philosophy is not the end of our relation to philosophy. Because both Hegel and Heidegger understand their thinking as taking place at the end of philosophy, there has been a tendency to interpret them, and especially Heidegger, so that the experience of the history of thinking appears as a release from that history, our being granted independence from it. But the experience of the history of philosophy is rather the point of reentry into it—for Hegel in the shape of the history of Spirit, for Heidegger as the destiny of Being. And yet these are very different because they each experience the 'end' of philosophy differently.

2. The End of Philosophy – and Its Beginning

The very different character that Hegel and Heidegger attribute to the end of philosophy is well reflected in—one might say, is dependent upon—their different assessments of the beginning of Western thinking. Hegel and Heidegger agree in attributing a seminal place to Parmenides' saying, *"to gar auto noein estin te kai einai,"* which is usually translated "Thinking and Being are the same." For Heidegger, it provides the basic theme for the whole of Western thinking. He says that "the history of that thinking is at bottom a sequence of variations on this one theme" (WD 148; tr. 242). This seems to echo Hegel's comment that this fragment is where genuine philosophizing began: "Its explanation constitutes the development of philosophy" (GP I 290; tr. 254). And when we look at their further comments on the fragment, the claim that Heidegger has in some way inverted Hegel's history of philosophy appears to be confirmed. For Hegel, philosophy is present only in its perfection, and the explanation of Parmenides' saying, which takes place in the very development of Western philosophy, is complete only in the perfection of philosophy. Hegel places so much value on that development that he judges that philosophy "is not yet present *(vorhanden)* here" in Parmenides' saying. For Heidegger, by contrast, the development of philosophy from this starting point almost has the character of a falling away. "The beginning is the strangest and mightiest. What comes afterwards is not the development but the flattening that results from mere spreading out; it is inability to retain the beginning" (EM 119; tr. 155). But what might apparently look like an inversion, whereby the progress of Hegel's history of Spirit becomes the decline of Heidegger's account of the growing oblivion of Being, is more complex. Neither Hegel nor Heidegger accords a one-sided privilege to either the beginning or the end. More important than any ideas of progress or decline is the fact that both Hegel and Heidegger agree that the thinking of Parmenides is not yet philosophy. But then how can Heidegger insist that his interpretation of what we know today as Parmenides' third fragment is utterly foreign to the approach of Hegel (VA 236; EGT 84)?

Just as Hegel believes that Parmenides' saying comes into its own only at the end of philosophy, so for Heidegger it remains unheard in some fundamental sense until the end of philosophy. Heidegger insists that the difference between his reading of the fragment and that given by Hegel lies in the different senses in which the two thinkers think "the end of philosophy." "All depends on whether the dialogue we have undertaken first of all and continually allows itself to respond to the questioning address of early thinking, or whether it simply closes itself off to such an address and cloaks early thought with the mantle of more recent doctrines" (VA 238-39; EGT 85). Otherwise said, it is a question of whether or not the early thinking of the Greeks is drawn into a region "dominated by the spheres of questioning of subsequent metaphysics." For Hegel the end of philosophy is the culmination of metaphysics in a thinking that is itself the fulfillment of metaphysics; for Heidegger the end of philosophy takes place in a thinking that is and is not metaphysical. This emerges in the 1964 essay "The End of Philosophy and the Task of Thinking" where in contrast to the notion of a highest perfection *(höchste Vollkommenheit)*, which presumably refers to Hegel's presentation of history as a progress from the imperfect to the perfect, Heidegger advances the word *Vollendung* to characterize the end of philosophy. The *Vollendung* is the place of gathering *(Versammlung)* (SD 63; BW 375).[7]

This gathering shows itself in the discovery of the unity of Western thinking whereby Parmenides' saying can be recognized in, for example, Hegel's speculative proposition "Being is thinking" (PG 39; PS 33) or Kant's "highest principle of all a priori synthetic judgements": "The conditions of the possibility of experience in general are at the same time conditions of the possibility of objects of experience."[8] What *gathering* means in Heidegger is reflected in his dictum that Parmenides cannot be interpreted in terms of Kant, whereas the reverse is both possible and necessary. "Though Kant says something absolutely different, his thinking moves nonetheless in the same (not the identical) sphere as the thinking of the Greek thinkers" (WD 149; tr. 243). But the interpretation that shows this only becomes "possible and necessary" at the time of the gathering. It thinks "something which it is no longer the matter of philosophy to think" (SD 71; BW 383); but at the same time it knows that it does not think it from "outside" philosophy (VA 72; EP 85). The issues are, first, whether the recognition of the gathering at the end of philosophy does not amount to the attainment of a privileged standpoint and, second, whether this insistence on the unity of metaphysics is not itself a reflection of the totalizing tendency of metaphysics. A third issue, the question of what might be understood by a thinking that is and yet is not metaphysical, underlies the whole of the present book and so must be postponed.

As to the first point, Heidegger maintains that there is no privileged standpoint at the end of philosophy, simply a different standpoint, one that is as much defined by what it lacks—a word for Being—as by its positive character (SD 66; BW 378). Certainly Hegel measures history from the standpoint of the present as the highest. But in Heidegger there is no basis for one epoch to pass judgement on another. He rejects the possibility of a comparison between the various epochs of philosophy (SD 62; BW 375). This is because Hegel and Heidegger understand the notion of "epoch" differently. In Hegel the epochs of history correspond to the principles in which Spirit has discovered itself; in Heidegger, whether the epochs within the history of philosophy or the history of philosophy as a single epoch is meant, "epoch" is always thought in terms of the holding back of Being.[9] But again these two notions of "epoch" are not simply mirror images of each other, the one in terms of revealing, the other in terms of concealing.

For Hegel philosophical insight into history takes the form of discovering the continuity *(Zusammenhang)* within the movement of epochs; this means gaining insight into the transitions between them. It is by discovering the necessity of its development and eliminating its contingency that Hegel's history fulfills itself and becomes a theodicy.[10] The introduction to the *Phenomenology of Spirit* explicates the dialectic as the power whereby the new object arises out of the old; the viewpoint of philosophy is that which sees this process at work. Although it is not a favorite word of his, we can say that Hegel provides an *explanation* of history—in terms of Spirit, reason, and the divine. It is entirely different with Heidegger. If epochs cannot be compared, then the growing oblivion of Being cannot be understood systematically. "The growing oblivion of Being" does not mean that with every great thinker, the oblivion of Being becomes increasingly more concealed. Metaphysics is as "essentially remote from the beginning in its start as in its finish" (NII 487; EP 81). Nor can the oblivion of Being serve as a principle of explanation, so long as we understand by *explanation* a referring of the unknown to the known. The oblivion of Being is in principle the unknown; the history of such oblivion is errancy. To be sure, the history of Being is not arbitrary; Heidegger says that each epoch has its own necessity (SD 62; BW 375). Quoted out of context this sentence seems to support the claim that Heidegger's history has a Hegelian structure. Restored to the text, where the issue is whether one epoch of metaphysics can be regarded as more perfect than another, it means rather that no one epoch is more necessary — or perfect — than another. Heidegger is raising the question whether Hegel, with his notion of progress *(Fortschritt)*, does not ultimately evade the *historical* nature of philosophy — notwithstanding his earlier statement that Hegel is the only Western thinker to have thoughtfully experienced the history of thinking.

In the 1962 lecture "Time and Being," Heidegger says that "the sequence of epochs in the destiny of Being is not accidental, nor can it be calculated as necessary" (SD 9; TB 9). In the protocol of a seminar devoted to the lecture, he restates this by saying that the transformation of epochs within metaphysics is a free sequence *(freie Folge)*. There is for Heidegger no "why," only the "that." Whereas for Hegel, historical necessity answers the question "why?", all that Heidegger can say is that "thinking can ascertain something like necessity in the sequence, something like an order and a consistency" (SD 56; TB 52). This tentativeness corresponds to Heidegger's account of the history of Being, where stages are listed in order, but where there is no pretence at completeness. Ultimately the necessity of Heidegger's history of Being is only the necessity of taking the step back to the beginning of thinking. That the sequence of the history of Being is "free" means that it is a discontinuous sequence. Being always occurs as an *excess* over what has gone before. The growing oblivion of Being is impenetrable: it lacks the coherence of Hegel's dialectical history, which allows one to explain retrospectively how the old gave birth to the new in a necessary sequence.

Hence there can be no *logic* of transitions *(Übergänge)* in Heidegger. The phrase "genuine transition," which does appear in the essay "Metaphysics as History of Being" (1941), might give the contrary impression and lead us to suppose a proximity to the transitions of the dialectic.[11] What Heidegger says is that "the ambiguity of the essence of actuality in the beginning of modern metaphysics is the sign of a genuine transition" (NII 428; EP 25). Heidegger's topic here is the transformation of actuality in modern metaphysics. He finds that there is no sudden and total change at the beginning of the modern epoch, as one might suppose is demanded by the idea of an epochal destiny of Being. The above sentence belongs to Heidegger's reply to the possible objection that the epochal view of history is in some way challenged by the coexistence of the modern conception of actuality alongside the old. Heidegger in reply concedes not only that the old and the new coexist, but also that at first no single conception emerges to challenge the old. The essence of Being at the beginning of modern metaphysics is, he says, ambiguous in the sense of having a multiplicity of meanings before seeming finally to decide upon one. This lack of a sweeping transformation is in keeping with the history of Being as a history of errancy. It might be different if the new conception of actuality were in some way established by argument, but it is a concealed destiny not subject to human ordering. For Heidegger, the ambiguity of the concept of actuality arises from the difficulty that essential thinking has in being genuine. Being does not simply, as it were, pass its judgement down; the thinker must listen to the destiny of Being and bring it to language. The phrase "genuine transition" in Heidegger has nothing to do with a dialectic of transitions.

3. Remembrance in Hegel and Heidegger

The second issue raised above was whether Heidegger's notions of completion *(Vollendung)* and "gathering" were not themselves metaphysical insofar as they ascribed a unity to metaphysics. If the presence of such a move could be identified in Heidegger, it could be argued that Heidegger's thinking exhibited a totalizing tendency of the kind familiar from Hegel and that his attempt to differentiate his own thinking from that of philosophy would collapse.

There is certainly no shortage of passages in which Heidegger seems to impute just such a unity to metaphysics. Many of these occur in the context of his attempt to display *a-letheia* at work in metaphysics, yet unthought by metaphysics. It is reflected also, for example, in the assertion quoted above that all Western thinking hitherto has been a sequence of variations on one theme. Is the gathering of metaphysics not its totalizing? Does not the experience of the end of philosophy necessarily constitute as a unity whatever preceded it? The answer is that such is the case only when thinking has in view the goal of either serving as the summation or interiorization of all previous thinking or of leaving it behind. Neither is the case for Heidegger. That Heidegger does not seek to turn his back on metaphysics is clear from the fact that his thinking proceeds by a constant dialogue with the thinking that precedes. That Heidegger's thinking is not to be understood as the culminating perfection of what has gone before under the name of philosophy, is apparent from a comparison of the word *Erinnerung* as it appears in both Hegel and Heidegger.

Erinnerung describes, both for Hegel and for Heidegger, the thinker's relation to the history of philosophy at the end of philosophy. It has usually been translated as *recollection*, but perhaps *remembrance* serves us better if it can somehow be heard as invested with less of a subjective connotation. To emphasize the sense of interiorizing, Hegel in the closing paragraph of the *Phenomenology of Spirit* hyphenates it: *Er-Innerung*. Nevertheless we are entirely misled about the meaning of the term in Hegel if we understand by it a making-inward of what is external. To be sure, we often think of education in those terms: something is given to us and we must make it our own, we must take possession of it. To this self-understanding of education as an inwardizing that raises to the universal Hegel gives the name *Bildung*, which may be translated as *culture* or, sometimes better, *formation*. He borrowed this term from the previous generation of German writers, but he found it inadequate to the task of describing the full complexity of our relation to the past. The individual is the result of Spirit and as such he inherits a past that is not external to him. What actually takes place in *Bildung*, although it is beyond the self-understanding of *Bildung* itself, is the realization of what in fact already belongs to us (PG 24–25; tr. 16–17).

Hegel finds evidence of this process, which we more properly call an actualization, in the ease with which what at one time was at the frontiers of knowledge is passed on to the children of later generations as commonplace. It was to meet this fact that Hegel developed the concept of the universal individual *(das allgemeine Individuum)*. This somewhat daunting phrase refers to the universal Spirit, the World-Spirit, to which the individual belongs as a child of his or her own times. As particular individuals, we have incorporated its wisdom; that is how progress is possible. Insofar as we not only raise this substantiality to consciousness through education, but also become aware, through an appreciation of history, that this is what is taking place, the *Weltgeist* becomes self-conscious Spirit, substance becomes subject. It is this latter process that gives rise to *begriffne Geschichte* as the gathering remembrance that Hegel calls *Er-Innerung*. This awareness of history, not as an indifferent externality, but as Spirit's own result, is attained only in absolute knowing, when Spirit knows itself as Spirit. *Er-Innerung* belongs to the final stage of this development.

In Heidegger also, *Erinnerung* belongs to a specific time. What comes to light in remembrance is not so much the unity of metaphysics as the persistence of the beginning as it prevails through all that follows. This is announced in the experience of the essence of technology that we shall examine in chapter 5. It is not accidental that the epoch of technology is the time of remembrance — or, as Heidegger also says, that technology is "completed metaphysics" (VA 80; EP 93). In modern technology, according to Heidegger, it seems as though man everywhere and always encounters only himself (VA 35; BW 308). This recalls Hegel's description of the element of philosophy as "pure self-recognition in absolute otherness" (PG 22; tr. 14). In Heidegger this self-reflection is not a perfection, but "the final delusion," for it is ignorant of technology as a challenge addressed to humanity (VA 38; BW 311).

What is crucial about the oblivion of Being understood through the experience of the essence of technology is how it looks not only backward, but also forward to another beginning: it has a Janus head (SD 57; TB 53). The experience of the end cannot be separated from the annunciation of another beginning. There are not two insights, one into the past as it belongs to the present, and another into the future as it comes toward us in the present: the future comes "as the imposition of the originating *(Anfängliche)*."[12] Remembrance is another way of thinking, a commemorative thinking *(andenkendes Denken)*. The change from manipulative thinking to this commemorative thinking cannot itself be manipulated. It is a change of mind that we do not bring about by changing our attitudes, but that we suffer. It takes place as the entry into the word's own rule, which means making the passage from concept-formation, as something over which we imagine that we have control, into placing ourselves within the grant of language.

This "retrogression to the word"[13] becomes, in Heidegger's thinking of the history of philosophy, the remembrance of "words for Being." Occasionally Heidegger presents lists of such words: *Physis, Logos, Hen, Idea, Energeia, Substantiality, Subjectivity, the Will, the Will to Power, the Will to Will* (ID 58; tr. 66). These are only examples; no such list is ever complete and it is sometimes forgotten that phrases like "der Satz vom Grund"—"nothing is without ground"—and Nietzsche's word "God is dead" are also "words of Being." Drawn from the realm of philosophy, they are words around which a philosopher's thinking appears to gather itself, even though Heidegger is at the same time prepared to concede that each thinker finds it hard to maintain himself in the word and seems at times almost to shy away from it. These words are heard by the thinker at the end of philosophy as words for Being precisely insofar as they still address us—even though ambiguously. This is why it would be wrong to think that, with the overcoming of metaphysics, we are closed off from the tradition. Rather, the end of philosophy allows us to hear anew the richness of previous thinking; that is the sense in which the future comes toward us as the imposition of the past. And, with the emergence of the words for Being, the history of philosophy announces itself as the history of Being.

At the close of his *Lectures on the History of Philosophy*, Hegel offers a summary of the results of the history of philosophy (GP III 461; tr. 552-53). Presented as results, they depart from the speculative presentation to which they properly belong, but they nevertheless serve as a valuable reference point for a comparison between Hegel and Heidegger. First, there is for Hegel only one philosophy in which Spirit completes its self-recognition; the different philosophies of the tradition emerge as the principles in which Spirit has discovered itself. For Heidegger, there is a unity to metaphysics that arises from the persistence of the concealed beginning and becomes visible only at its end; but this 'unity' shows itself as a sequence of different historical words for Being unrecognized as such until that end. Second, the sequence of philosophies has for Hegel a necessity visible retrospectively from the absolute standpoint. For

Heidegger, the sequence is free, takes place in a series of ruptures, and remains in principle impenetrable. Third, the final philosophy of a period is, for Hegel, the result of the progressive development of truth. The most recent philosophy contains what preceded it and is its product. For Heidegger, remembrance takes place from another beginning. The notion of another beginning implies a different relation to the first beginning from that found in Hegel. So for Hegel, the beginning as it takes place in Parmenides takes the form of a "not yet" that is left behind; whereas for Heidegger, the "not yet" of the beginning is precisely that of a future that arises only after metaphysics has passed in between. It is Parmenides' word *aletheia* that serves for Heidegger as this "not-yet" and Hegel's silence about *aletheia* is his answer to the question posed in *Basic Problems of Phenomenology* as to whether Hegel exhausted all the possibilities of the beginning of philosophy.

> In Hegel, philosophy—that is, ancient philosophy—is in a certain sense thought through to its end. He was completely in the right when he himself expressed this consciousness. But there exists just as much the legitimate demand to start anew, to understand the finiteness of the Hegelian system and to see that Hegel himself has come to an end with philosophy because he moves in the circle of philosophical problems.[14]

That statement is misleading only if the suggestion that Hegel's thinking has come to an end were taken to suggest that our reading of it was complete. For Heidegger, the provocation to think again takes places through the dialogue with previous thinking that—as he says in the context of an essay on Parmenides— never comes to an end (VA 256; EGT 100-101). In the case of his continual rereading of Hegel, this call to another beginning shows itself—as we shall see in the final chapter—in the recognition of Hegel's word *experience* as a word for Being.[15]

NOTES

1. See especially *Identität und Differenz*, pp. 107-43; trans. J. Stambaugh, *Identity and Difference*, pp. 42-74. "Hegel und die Griechen," *Wegmarken*, pp. 255-72. *Zur Sache des Denkens*, pp. 51-56; trans. J. Stambaugh, *On Time and Being*, pp. 47-52. *Heraklit*, (Frankfurt: Klostermann, 1970); trans. C. H. Seibert, *Heraclitus Seminar 1966/67* (University, Ala.: University of Alabama Press, 1979).

2. H-G. Gadamer/*Wahrheit und Methode*, (Tübingen: J. C. B. Mohr, 1960); trans. W. Glen-Doepel *Truth and Method* (London: Sheed & Ward, 1975 and New York: Seabury, 1976).

3. *Wahrheit und Methode*, p. 286; trans. *Truth and Method*, p. 269. See also Rüdiger Bubner's *Modern German Philosophy* (New York and Cambridge; Cambridge University Press, 1981), pp. 60-68, and my review in *Ratio*, 1983, pp. 171-178.

4. Suspicions of this kind had been raised by Karl Löwith in 1962: "Heideggers Vorlesungen über Nietzsche," *Aufsätze und Vorträge 1930-1970* (Stuttgart: Kohlhammer, 1971). See now especially Michel Haar, "Structures hégéliennes dans la pensée heideggérienne de l'Histoire," *Revue de Métaphysique et de Morale* 85, no. 1 (1980):48-59.

5. Aristotle, *De Anima* 1. 1, ii. 403b20-7; trans. W. S. Hett *On the Soul* (London: Heinemann, and Cambridge: Harvard University Press, 1964), p. 18.

6. *Die Grundprobleme der Phänomenologie*, Gesamtausgabe Band 24, hrsg. F-W. von Herrmann (Frankfurt: Klostermann, 1975), p. 400; trans. A. Hofstadter, *The Basic Problems of Phenomenology* (Bloomington, Ind.: Indiana University Press, 1982), p. 282. Whether "the end of philosophy" is meant here already in Heidegger's own sense, or whether it is still used in Hegel's sense, is a question I shall return to in section 3 of this chapter and again in chapter 6, section 2.

7. Heidegger had, certainly since the sketch "Metaphysics as History of Being" (1941), used the word *Versammlung* to refer to the play of concealing-unconcealing that is *aletheia* (NII 420; EP 19). This sense is uppermost in "The End of Philosophy and the Task of Thinking," but consideration of *aletheia* has been reserved to chapter 2 below. This is the sense in which the end of philosophy is the entry into the region *(Gegend)* or clearing *(Lichtung)*. It should be noted also that Heidegger understands death as a gathering (H 280; PLT 126). A basis for talking of the "death of philosophy" could be found in Heidegger, though it would be an understanding quite different from that in which the phrase is usually used.

8. *Kritik der reinen Vernunft* A 158, B 197; trans. N. Kemp Smith *Critique of Pure Reason* (London: Macmillan, 1929), p. 194. Heidegger's Kant interpretations remained constant in affirming this as the central sentence. His reading was concerned with showing how Being as the objectivity of the object and thinking as the forming of ideas concerning the Being of empirical beings, could not be separated. The relation with Parmenides is most clearly stated in "Kants These über das Sein," *Wegmarken*, p. 304; trans. Ted E. Klein and William E. Pohl, "Kant's Thesis about Being," *Southwestern Journal of Philosophy* 4 (1973), p. 31. (See also WD 148; tr. 242.)

9. *Vorlesungen über die Philosophie der Weltgeschichte*, Band 1, *Die Vernunft in der Geschichte*, hrsg. J. Hoffmeister (Hamburg: Meiner, 1970), p. 75; trans. H. Nisbett, *Lectures on the Philosophy of World History* (New York and Cambridge: Cambridge University Press, 1975), p. 131. *Vorlesungen über die Geschichte der Philosophie* p. 457; trans. *Lectures on the History of Philosophy*, 3:548. *Holzwege*, p. 311; trans. *Early Greek Thinking*, pp. 26-27. *Zur Sache des Denkens*, p. 9; trans. *On Time and Being*, p. 9. Cf. M. Haar, "Structures hégéliennes dans la pensée heideggérienne de l'Histoire," p. 54.

10. E.g., *Die Vernunft in der Geschichte*, p. 48; trans. *Philosophy of World History*, p. 42.

11. Reference is made to this passage by Michel Haar, "Structures hégéliennes dans la pensée heideggérienne de l'Histoire," p. 56.

12. "Grundsätze des Denkens," *Jahrbuch für Psychologie und Psychotherapie* 6 (1958): 35; trans. J. Hart and J. Maraldo, *The Piety of Thinking* (Bloomington, Ind.: Indiana University Press, 1976), p. 48.

13. "Der Rückgang auf das Wort." The phrase is Beda Allemann's from *Hölderlin und Heidegger* (Freiburg: Atlantis, 1954), pp. 115-17. What I say at the end of the paragraph about "hearing anew the richness of previous thought" will be clarified and qualified later, particularly in chapter 4.

14. *Die Grundprobleme der Phänomenologie*, p. 400; *The Basic Problems of Phenomenology*, p. 282.

15. That the dialogue with Hegel is opened up, rather than closed off, is also evident from the recognition of *Versammlung* or "gathering" at work *transmuted* in Hegel's concept of dialectic. *Holzwege*, pp. 161-69; trans. *Hegel's Concept of Experience* (New York: Harper & Row, 1970), pp. 105-19. Also *Wegmarken*, p. 258. These are examples of what Heidegger had already in 1927 called the "appropriation" *(Aneignung)* of Hegel. *Die Grundprobleme der Phänomenologie*, p. 25; trans. *The Basic Problems of Phenomenology*, p. 178.

Chapter Two
Aletheia and the
Concealment of Concealing

1. Truth and Unconcealment

In "The Onto-theo-logical Constitution of Metaphysics," a lecture dating from 1957, Heidegger attempts to characterize the difference between Hegel's conversation with the history of philosophy and his own. For Hegel, this character is *Aufhebung*, understood as a negating that at the same time preserves, and Heidegger emphasizes how it leads to "the heightening and gathering area of absolute posited truth in the sense of the completely developed certainty of self-knowing knowledge." Heidegger characterizes his own thinking as the step back to the realm, hitherto passed over, from which the essence of truth first becomes worthy of thought (ID 39; tr. 49). The step back, he says, goes from what is unthought, the difference between Being and beings, to what gives us thought, what calls for thinking, the oblivion of the difference. This oblivion is to be thought in terms of *lethe*, the Greek word for concealment.

One year later, in 1958, Heidegger delivered the lecture "Hegel and the Greeks" in which he attempted to make more specific the difference between his own work and that of Hegel in respect of the history of philosophy. He observed that Hegel, whose concept of truth as the absolute certainty of the self-knowing subject is at the most extreme distance from the Greek experience, fails to focus on *aletheia* in his presentation of the history of philosophy. The difference between *Erinnerung* in Hegel and Heidegger can now be clarified further by pointing to the former's incapacity to think *aletheia*. *Aletheia* is the unthought as such (W 272). And yet this means that *aletheia* pervades all thought, persisting through metaphysics, unheard until its end. This is the sense in which Heidegger can say, in spite of his claim that Hegel fails to think *aletheia*, that nevertheless *aletheia* pervades Hegel's *Phenomenology of Spirit* transmuted (VA 183; PLT 185).

Heidegger's own concentration on the theme of *aletheia* had begun in lectures delivered over thirty years earlier. Then, in *Being and Time*, combining historical and phenomenological investigation, he accompanied his description of the way

15

assertions are confirmed with an interpretation of the Greek word *aletheia*. Unconcealment is the primordial phenomenon of truth. The traditional conception of truth as an *adaequatio* or correspondence of understanding and thing arises in Avicenna[1] but it presupposes, and thus could be shown to derive from, the Greek notion of truth as unconcealment. This is shown first by phenomenological description: only if the thing shows itself, can there by a comparison between understanding and thing. Then, returning to the Greeks, Heidegger recalls two passages from the first book of Aristotle's *Metaphysics* where Parmenides is described first as compelled to follow what showed itself in itself, the phenomena, and secondly as compelled by *aletheia* itself (SZ 213; tr. 256). Heidegger recognizes the similarity between these two statements and on the basis of a combination of evidence of this kind, he comes to regard the conventional translation of *aletheia* as "truth" as inadequate; he prefers the word "uncoveredness" *(Entdecktheit)* (SZ 220; tr. 263). The uncoveredness of beings, their discovery, is then referred back to the disclosure *(Erschlossenheit)* of *Dasein*, which had already been described in section 18 of the book and to which the name *Lichtung* had been given in section 28. In thus laying bare the ontological foundation of truth in the sense of *aletheia* and *adaequatio*, Heidegger emphasizes that he has not "shaken off" the tradition, but appropriated it *(Aneignung)* more primordially (SZ 220; tr. 262).

In saying that *Dasein* was what was primarily "true," in the sense of uncovering (SZ 222; tr. 265), Heidegger goes a step further than could easily be maintained on a basis of a reading of the Greek texts. Indeed, we are liable today to underestimate the novelty of his translation of *aletheia* as "unconcealment," because of the influence it has had on Greek scholarship, particularly in Germany. But in *Being and Time*, Heidegger reads *aletheia* as a privative expression — as *a-letheia* — so that the Greek privative alpha is taken to indicate that unconcealment always takes the form of "a kind of robbery" (SZ 222; tr. 265). This formulation could be misunderstood and the later essay "On the Essence of Truth" is careful to clarify it (W 89; BW 132). Concealment is not simply opposed to unconcealment as if beings were snatched from the truth, as *Being and Time* puts it; concealment always accompanies unconcealment. In fact, that much had already been recognized in *Being and Time* itself, where uncovering and hiding belong together in *a-letheia* in the same way that thrownness and projection belong together in the thrown project *(geworfene Entwurf)* (SZ 223; tr. 265). But if *a-letheia* was to serve as the title for what remained unthought in metaphysics, another characterization of it would need to be developed.[2]

Both *Being and Time* and "On the Essence of Truth" (my reading of which I shall postpone to chapter 5) appear to be attempts to pursue a transcendental inquiry into the nature of truth in the sense of investigating the conditions of its possibility. They both present themselves, in the first instance, as retrogressive analyses on the way to a more primordial conception. Both works indicate that such an inquiry might, in some unclarified sense, reverse the historical development which led to truth being identified with the correspondence theory of truth. This is most apparent in *Being and Time*. Along with the claim that the unconcealment of beings—and thus ultimately of *Dasein*—makes possible the correctness of assertions, we find the historical thesis that the Greek conception of *aletheia* stands behind the development in the Middle Ages of the *adaequatio* theory. There is a clear implication that the two inquiries necessary to establish both these claims are mutually supporting. It is tempting to see "On the Essence of Truth" as pursuing the first of these tasks and the essay "Plato's Doctrine of Truth," which was written over much the same period, as taking up the historical investigation.[3] What the appropriation of *aletheia* amounts to and what the conditions were that made such an appropriation possible are questions answered at the time of *Being and Time* by reference to the notion of "the destruction of the history of ontology" (SZ 19-27; tr. 41-49). But *Being and Time* lacked, as Heidegger subsequently conceded, a genuine understanding of what he called "the history of Being" (VS 133). The remainder of this chapter is devoted to an investigation of how the insight into the history of Being is reflected in the reading Heidegger subsequently offers of the word *aletheia*.

2. An Ambiguity in Plato

The essay "Plato's Doctrine of Truth" is of particular interest not only for its focus on *aletheia*, but also because it is Heidegger's most sustained attempt to detail an historical transition. Here he seems at first reading to be concerned, for once, not with identifying the word for Being in the language of a thinker, so much as substantiating the claim that a change in the essence of truth takes place "unsaid" in Plato's work. He proceeds through an exposition of the allegory of the cave from book 6 of *The Republic*. The change in the determination of truth is from *aletheia* (unconcealment) to *orthotes* (correctness). It takes place in the subordination of *aletheia* to the *idea*. He even attempts to pinpoint this in a particular sentence where Plato says, according to Heidegger's own translation, that the Idea of the good, the *agathon*, "is itself master, dispensing both unhiddenness (to what emerges) and the ability to perceive (the unhidden)."[4] When the essence of truth relinquishes the basic feature of unhiddenness and becomes correctness, the site of truth ceases to be beings themselves and becomes one's stance toward beings. Truth becomes the likeness *(homoiosis)* between what is said in an assertion and a state of affairs; the way forward to the familiar definition of truth as an *adaequatio* has been prepared for, even if it has not yet been attained (W 138; P 188). Indeed, at the end of "Plato's Doctrine of Truth," Heidegger emphasizes the further transformations that the essence of truth underwent after Plato. He mentions Aquinas, Descartes, and Nietzsche. Nietzsche's definition of truth as a kind of error is called the last reflection of the sequence, its unconditional "fulfillment" (Vollendung), the same word Heidegger uses to describe the end of philosophy (SD 62; BW 374).

The change in the essence of truth in Plato is said to initiate the history of metaphysics. In this context, Heidegger offers an expression that suggests that he conceives this history as governed by continuity. He says that the change in the essence of truth is present as the all-penetrating basic actuality, long since established and still undisturbed. The impression is emphasized by his use of the image of the world history of the globe rolling on into modernity (W 142-43; P 191). But recognition of the sense in which the past is present through continuity only takes place through the past becoming present in Erinnerung. It is only in the remembrance that takes place at the end of metaphysics that the unity of metaphysics comes to light as that from which we are separated. Remembrance finds that in Plato unhiddenness is subordinated to idea. This describes a change not in the definition of truth, but in the destiny of the Being of beings. The "rolling on of world history" is referred through Erinnerung to the history of Being. The subordination of aletheia to the idea of the good means that agathon is taken as a name for Being: agathon is a granting through which beings are held together in Being (W 135; P 186). Already at the time of the first publication of "Plato's Doctrine of Truth," Heidegger was expressing severe reservations about the phrase "transformation of the essence of truth." The phrase was an expedient; it speaks of truth objectively and not of the way in which it unfolds (west).[5] The phrase "transformation of the essence of truth" suggests that Heidegger is concerned with variations of the definition of truth as if truth was somehow given in advance as a permanent essence. But this is precisely not the case. Heidegger in 1967, looking back on his attempt to think aletheia, begun some forty-five years earlier, states this very clearly. He says in the course of a seminar on Heraclitus that Being and Time was already moving in the direction of thinking aletheia so that it had nothing to do with truth, but that in the meantime 'truth' had intervened.[6] We have to read the essay so that it is not primarily about truth, but about Being. Aletheia may have nothing to do with truth, but truth has everything to do with aletheia. In "Plato's Doctrine of Truth" Heidegger does not fall prey to positing truth as somehow given in advance, but instead aletheia takes that position. The assertion that aletheia falls into oblivion at the beginning of metaphysics implies that prior to metaphysics, prior to Plato, it was not concealed. This assertion becomes problematic.

In the essay, "The End of Philosophy and the Task of Thinking," written in 1964 and first published—in French—in 1966, Heidegger made some comments that relate directly to this issue.

In the scope of this question [the question of how truth is granted only in the element of the clearing of presence], we must acknowledge the fact that *aletheia*, unconcealment in the sense of the clearing of presence, was originally experienced only as *orthotes*, as the correctness of representations and statements. But then the assertion about the essential transformation of truth, that is, from unconcealment to correctness, is also untenable. (SD 78; BW 390)

At first sight this statement looks like a straightforward retraction of the essay on Plato and that is certainly how most commentators have taken it. The essay on Plato has always attracted a great deal of attention from Greek scholars eager to show that Heidegger's reading of Plato is inadequate, but there has been a surprising lack of concern among Heidegger scholars to assess the implications of the retraction, if indeed it is one.[7] References to a change in the essence of truth abound in Heidegger's writings and do not constitute a doctrine that could be readily isolated or bracketed from Heidegger's *corpus*. We shall find that if we restore the passage in question to its original context and if at the same time we consider further references Heidegger makes to the Plato essay, then the picture becomes more complex, so that we shall be forced to adopt a different interpretation.

In the passage quoted, Heidegger is referring to the extended controversy surrounding his interpretation of *aletheia* as unconcealment. The principal antagonist was Paul Friedländer who had been at Marburg when Heidegger was there in the 1920s and who ended his career as professor of classics at the University of California. The second German edition of his book on Plato, published in 1954, contained in its first volume a chapter opposing Heidegger's interpretation of Plato's conception of truth. This book formed the basis for the first English edition of the work published four years later, although Friedländer took the opportunity to rework the discussion, in particular to incorporate Hesiod's use of *alethes* in the privative sense of *a-lethes*, albeit in respect of a person. The third German edition, which was published in 1964, was largely unchanged except that the chapter that dealt with Heidegger's interpretation of *aletheia* had undergone substantial revision. The third German edition formed the basis for the second English edition of 1969, except that Friedländer, before his death in 1968, used the opportunity to revise his discussion of Heidegger once more. There are therefore some four different versions of Friedländer's case against Heidegger.[8]

The first two versions of the chapter had amounted to an unrestrained attack on Heidegger. When he revised it in 1964 and 1968, Friedländer reaffirmed his opposition to Heidegger's interpretation of Plato, but his conclusion was accompanied by certain important concessions:

In my discussion with Martin Heidegger, I have learned that my earlier opposition to the interpretation of *aletheia* as unhiddenness was unjustified. What stands unchanged is my criticism of Heidegger's historical construction. For the result has become even more clear. It was not "first in Plato" that truth became the correctness of perception and assertion. This meaning was present much earlier, i.e., in the old epic. For Plato, there is in *alethes* and *aletheia* an equilibrium between the revealing truth, the unhidden reality, and the truthfulness which measures that reality by this truth. Plato did not corrupt the concept of *aletheia*, as Heidegger claims. Plato sharpened the concept, systematized it, and heightened it.[9]

In the first version of his attack on Heidegger's interpretation Friedländer had made a great deal of the word's etymology, opposing quite stringently the derivation of *aletheia* from *lethe* preceded by the privative *alpha*. But he could not fail to be impressed by the number of scholars who came to Heidegger's defense and in the revised version he conceded that his opposition to the various etymological interpretations of the word *aletheia* had been unfounded. The extent to which his revised criticisms changed ground are concealed in the version: "It remains true (1) that *alethes* and *aletheia* were perhaps originally not negatives and (2) that they were never felt to be pure negatives." This first claim marks a striking change of tone from his earlier attack and indeed from the second claim, which is surely no easier to prove than the etymological case he is opposing.

In 1958 Heidegger, in the essay "Hegel and the Greeks," responded briefly to the criticisms Friedländer had made four years earlier. In particular he addressed Friedländer's emphasis on the fact that, with only one exception, *aletheie* and *alethes* appear in Homer attached to verbs of saying. At this time Heidegger asked whether this in itself proves anything; language perhaps also resides under the sway of unconcealment (W 271 and VS 73-74). Friedländer never responded to this possibility; throughout he tended to consider Heidegger's claim as confined to the unconcealment of beings. In the 1964 essay Heidegger took up the point again. He conceded that *aletheia* "is often and justifiably used by Homer only in the *verba dicendi*, in statement and thus in the sense of correctness and reliability, not in the sense of unconcealment" (SD 77; BW 389). Meanwhile Friedländer pointed to a passage in *The Iliad* where *alethes* is used not in connection with an assertion, but to call a spinning woman "honest or reliable" (bk. 12, line 433). Elsewhere in *The Iliad* the word is used in such a way that he is even prepared to concede that the context suggests that unhiddenness, rather than the correctness of the assertion is meant (bks. 6, line 382 and 23, line 361). The further objection in Friedländer's first attack, that Heidegger's account of truth as unconcealment is subjective, disappeared altogether after 1958 (Cf. W 270).

Heidegger's response to the fact that he appeared to be winning the etymological argument is striking. Friedländer surely exaggerated when he supposed that etymology was the basis for Heidegger's far-reaching conclusions. In *Being and Time*, Heidegger does indeed draw on the linguistic evidence and there is furthermore every reason to believe that listening to the word and letting it speak contributed to the discovery that concealment belongs to unconcealment. But Heidegger's reading of *a-letheia* was never simply a thesis that could have been established at the level of an argument about language. Seeking to distance himself from etymological arguments, Heidegger says that "it is not for the sake of etymology that I stubbornly translate the name *aletheia* as unconcealment...." (SD 75–76; BW 388). Heidegger is at such pains to concede to Friedländer the philological evidence and consequently the question of the alleged change in the concept of truth, not in order to abandon the fundamental place of *aletheia* in his thinking, but, as we shall see, so as to maintain it the more strongly. In other words, Heidegger emphasizes the difference between what is discovered by historical scholarship on the one hand and what is granted to remembrance on the other. The philological argument must of necessity be concerned with, for example, the question of whether *aletheia* was originally understood as bearing an alpha privative, but such an argument was not sufficiently far-reaching. When Heidegger hyphenated *a-letheia* in his later writings, he was not concerned to establish such a reading. Heidegger does not disregard such evidence as bears on his claims; but particularly in his later writings, what he was saying was not open to confirmation or rejection according to such evidence.

Nevertheless Friedländer did not relax his objections to Heidegger's reading of Plato. Because truth in the sense of the correctness of perception and assertion is present prior to Plato, Friedländer denies the claim that a transformation in the concept of truth in favor of correctness takes place in Plato. Friedländer is outraged by Heidegger's insistence that there is an ambiguity in Plato's account of truth:[10] Plato is rather to be commended for sharpening the concept of truth. We should be clear on the major point of difference between Friedländer and Heidegger. Although Friedländer disputes that there is such an ambiguity or *Zweideutigkeit*, he is nevertheless prepared to concede that there is a 'two-sidedness' or *Zweiseitigkeit* in Plato's discussion of truth, which he also refers to as an 'equilibrium' between two different conceptions of truth, as in the passage quoted above. What seems to offend Friedländer primarily is the suggestion that Plato's philosophical rigor is under attack. But it is not the case that Heidegger views the history of thinking as a decline from the recognition of *aletheia*, whereby Plato would be something less than his predecessors. Heidegger is not seeking to impugn Plato by the attribution of this ambiguity. Ambiguity is the sign of a genuine transition in the history of Being, as another essay from the same time puts it (NII 428; EP 25).

Heidegger's point is that this ambiguity was the mark of Plato's engagement in the saying of Being, as can be seen if we look more closely at his discussion of it. The ambiguity is apparent in the juxtaposition of two sayings about the idea of the good. At one point Plato uses the phrase *kuria aletheian kai noun* ("master dispensing both unconcealment and perceiving"). Elsewhere we find the phrase *panton orthon te kai kalon aitia* ("the first cause [i.e., the possibility of essence] of all that is correct as well as all that is beautiful"). Heidegger does not understand these two phrases so that "unconcealment" in the first corresponds to "correctness" in the other. Rather "correctness" corresponds to "perceiving" and "unconcealment" to "the beautiful." But whereas there is a likeness *(homoiosis)* between perceiving and correctness, the relation between unconcealment and the beautiful is one of discordance (W 137-38; P 188). Indeed this discordance is an unveiling of Being (NI 218-31; Ni 188-99).

This then is the context to which we must refer the statement that from the beginning *aletheia* was experienced as *orthotes*. Because insufficient attention has been given to that context, the statement has so far tended only to spread misunderstanding. Gadamer, for example, takes up Heidegger's "self-correction" and attempts to argue against him that, far from it being the case that Plato went along with the restriction of the experience of *aletheia* solely to correctness, he attempted with the idea of the Good "to think the realm of unconcealment."[11] But this simply shows how misled even such a distinguished reader of Heidegger could become; for Heidegger was not denying that Plato thought *aletheia* as unconcealment. In his retraction, Heidegger is concerned to dispel two incidental claims about the understanding of truth prior to Plato suggested by the essay: first, that *aletheia* was not yet thought in terms of correctness and, second, that in consequence the realm of unconcealment was luminous to all (W 137; P 187). But the retraction does not amount to a denial that in Plato *aletheia* as unconcealment — and thus also *orthotes* as correctness — comes under the yoke of the *idea*. Once this is recognized, it becomes apparent that Heidegger's so-called retraction amounts to a strengthening and clarifying of his major claim concerning the concealment of concealing, not a weakening of it. The claim that there is, by means of the destiny of Being, an unfolding of the essence of *truth*, is not denied; but the emphasis has shifted away from a discussion couched in terms of the transformation of the essence of truth, a notion he had come to see as inadequate. In its place, greater emphasis was to be placed on the saying of Being as it takes place in Plato with the word *idea*. Heidegger's admission that the early Greeks did not think *aletheia* as *a-letheia* or as *Lichtung* is important, not because it leads to a denial of the ambiguity of Plato's allegory of the cave, but because it introduces another ambiguity, that between *aletheia* and *a-letheia*. The recognition of this ambiguity is already foreshadowed in the essay 'Plato's Doctrine of Truth' insofar as it knows that the reading given there is to be understood in terms of remembrance, and specifically a remembrance that has to think of the essence of truth more originally (W 143; P 192). What remains unsaid in Plato is not a shift in the definition of the essence of truth (W 109; P 173), but in *aletheia* as *a-letheia*. Yet that still leaves unclarified what *a-letheia* means when it serves as the title for what is unthought in metaphysics.

3. Heidegger's Rereading of His Essay on Plato

The distinction between the question of truth and the question of *aletheia* must be brought to play in rereading Heidegger's essay "Plato's Doctrine of Truth." There are, as it were, two essays to be found in *Wegmarken* under the title *Platons Lehre von der Wahrheit*. One is an essay primarily about the change in the conception of truth; it has received a great deal of attention – and not only from Friedländer. The other essay finds the question of a change in the essence of truth subordinated to the question of the history of Being, a history that can only be recovered by remembrance from the end of philosophy. Heidegger in "The End of Philosophy and the Task of Thinking" is proposing a way of reading his Plato essay; he is not withdrawing it altogether. He accomplishes this by distinguishing between the two questions of *aletheia* and of truth (SD 77; BW 389). The question of truth in this instance takes the form of asking "how truth, that is, the correctness of statements, is granted only in the element of the clearing of presence" (SD 78; BW 390). To be sure, this is a question that is not asked by philosophy; indeed, it is, as we shall see in chapter 5, a question raised – though also itself put in question – by the essay "On the Essence of Truth." Anyway, the supposed repudiation of the essay on Plato follows the question immediately: "In the scope of this question," that is, the question of truth, "we must acknowledge the fact that *aletheia*, unconcealment in the sense of the opening of presence, was originally only experienced as *orthotes*, as the correctness of representations and statements." But only two pages earlier, Heidegger had said that Parmenides had experienced *aletheia*, unconcealment. Those commentators who are in such a hurry to see Heidegger as having repudiated the essay on Plato, should ask first how this statement about Parmenides might be reconciled with their understanding of the remarks on *aletheia* as confined to correctness. To answer this question they will need to distinguish, as Heidegger does, natural experience, the experience of thinkers like Parmenides and Plato, and finally what still remained unthought by the Greeks in those experiences.

In "The End of Philosophy and the Task of Thinking" Heidegger asks how it is that *aletheia* appears to man's *natural* experience and speech solely as correctness and dependability (SD 78; BW 390). The answer is given only tentatively, in the form of a question, but its implications are nevertheless clear. "Does it happen because self-concealing, concealment *(lethe)*, belongs to *a-letheia*, not just as an addition, not as shadow to light, but rather as the heart of *aletheia*?" When Heidegger writes here *a-letheia* instead of *aletheia* it is not to draw attention to its possible etymology. The *lethe* is the oblivion of Being which belongs to metaphysics. Although the word is uttered by Parmenides at the beginning, it is heard only at the end of metaphysics when the question of Being is raised once again. To be sure, it is no longer raised as it was once raised at the beginning of metaphysics. It is now only raised as itself questionable in its inability to speak to us: "Are we nowadays even perplexed at our inability to understand the expression 'Being'?...This question [the question of Being] has today been forgotten" (SZ 1-2; tr. 19-21). It is the recovery at the end of philosophy of the question of Being—even in this muted form—that allows us to hear *aletheia* not as correctness but as echoing the oblivion of Being that passed between Parmenides and our own time. Only insofar as we ask the question of *aletheia*, not the question of truth, do we enter into this remembrance.

In two seminars in which Heidegger subsequently participated, he took up again the questions posed in "The End of Philosophy and the Task of Thinking." In the first, a seminar at Le Thor in 1969, he returned to the question of the oblivion of *aletheia*. It was because the first and decisive understanding of *aletheia* was in terms of the *aletheia* of the *logos* that the possibility to think *aletheia* as *a-letheia* was blocked (VS 74). In this way he showed that although philology did not of itself have access to the realm which thinking occupies at the end of philosophy, he nevertheless did not want to ignore the evidence that philology had provided; rather, he sought to integrate it. Nevertheless it should be noted that this clarification does not compromise the claim about the transformation of the essence of truth; Heidegger is here exploring the concealment of concealing that pervades Western thinking from its beginning. In the second, held in 1973 at Zähringen, he returned to the question of the place of Parmenides in respect of the thinking of *aletheia*. Taking up the question from "The End of Philosophy and the Task of Thinking," quoted above, in which he asks whether the *lethe* that belongs to *a-letheia* is not the heart of *aletheia*, Heidegger denied that Parmenides said anything of the kind.[12] Parmenides does not speak about the *lethe*, but about the presencing of presencing, both in respect of the experience and what it grants. Again, Heidegger's comment seems not to be a revision of what he had published in 1966, so much as the correction of a possible misreading. Read carefully, Heidegger had not said that Parmenides had thought *a-letheia* as such. Parmenides names *aletheia*, but this is not the last word, simply the first, said when metaphysics was "not yet." Only when metaphysics is "no longer" is *aletheia* thought as *a-letheia*. There is a kinship between the not-yet metaphysical and the no-longer metaphysical; this kinship arises because the latter listens to what is unsaid in what Parmenides says. Parmenides says *aletheia* and *a-letheia* is heard. It is because metaphysics has passed in between that the word now speaks differently and the concealment of Being within metaphysics comes to be heard from beyond metaphysics.

These formulations are not without their problems, problems that will have to be explored in the following chapters. First, it might seem that *a-letheia*, insofar as it is first heard at the time of the end of philosophy, is something new. It is crucial that for Heidegger *a-letheia* is the "oldest of the old" (SD 25; TB 24). The *lethe* at the heart of *aletheia* is not a subsequent addition that we bring to the word simply because it was not part of Parmenides' intention in using it. To meet the demands made by such a claim, Heidegger introduced into his thinking the word *trace (Spur)*, a notion that is developed particularly in the course of reading Hölderlin. It is also prominent in an essay on the Anaximander Fragment.[13]

> Oblivion of Being belongs to the self-veiling essence of Being.... This means that the history of Being begins with the oblivion of Being, since Being— together with its essence, its distinction from beings—keeps to itself.... Even the early trace of the distinction is obliterated when presencing appears as something present and finds itself in the position of being the highest being present. (H 336; EGT 50-51)

And yet it is only through the trace that has been left in language that at the end of philosophy, under conditions that we shall be exploring, the oblivion of Being can appear as concealed in language. In his late essays on language Heidegger explored the concealment of concealing that has left its trace in all language. This is particularly true of *aletheia*, as one of the early words of thinking. That concealment is traced graphically when we read the word as *a-letheia* should not be confused with an assertion about what Parmenides might have meant. When we hear the *lethe* in *aletheia* we are listening not to Parmenides, but to the speaking of language itself.

The second series of problems that arise from the formulations I have offered above, are provoked particularly by the suggestion that Heidegger passes *beyond* metaphysics or in some way leaves metaphysics "behind."[14] So long as these phrases are taken one-sidedly, they are inadequate. To claim to be "outside" metaphysics is not only to situate oneself in opposition to metaphysics, it is to do so according to the metaphysical distinction between the inside and the outside. Heidegger is more careful. Writing in 1943 in the postscript to "What is Metaphysics?", he says of the question about the ground of metaphysics that "such a question must think metaphysically and, at the same time, think in terms of the ground of metaphysics, i.e., no longer metaphysically. All such questions must remain ambiguous in an essential sense" (W 100; EB 382). This is reflected in the phrase that later provided the title for the introduction to "What is Metaphysics?"—"The Way Back into the Ground of Metaphysics." "The step back" could only be taken insofar as one had stepped "outside" and yet it has to be understood that insofar as there was any step "outside" it was only maintained by "stepping back" (inside). The word *remembrance*

(Erinnerung), which Heidegger also used to characterize his relation to the philosophical tradition, must equally be understood in terms of the essentially ambiguous stance of the thinker at the "end" of philosophy. It is an ambiguity that is to be found in all language insofar as it is read according to the question of Being. Just as Parmenides' word resounds with the ambiguity of *aletheia* and *a-letheia* whereby it is both metaphysical and not-yet metaphysical, so an ambiguity may be traced in Plato's text—and even in the thinking that traces it.[15] The ambiguity between *aletheia* and *a-letheia* that resounds in Parmenides also emerges as traced in Plato's text.

NOTES

1. Heidegger, following Aquinas, mistakenly attributes the *adaequatio* theory of truth to Isaac Israeli, *Sein und Zeit*, p. 214; trans. J. Macquarrie and E. Robinson, *Being and Time*, p. 257. Thomas Aquinas, *Quaestiones Disputatae* I. *De Veritate*, qu. 1, art. 1 (Turin: Marietti, 1964), p. 3; trans. R. Mulligan, *The Disputed Questions on Truth* qu. 1, art. 1 (Chicago; Regnery, 1952), p. 7. See A. Altmann and S. Stern, *Isaac Israeli* (Westport: Greenwood, 1979), p. 58-59.

2. Such a reading of *a-letheia* is indicated by the following sentence from "On the Essence of Truth": "The concealment of beings as a whole, untruth proper, is older than every openness of this or that being," *Wegmarken*, p. 89; trans. *Basic Writings*, p. 132. See Chapter 5 below.

3. "On the Essence of Truth" had its origin in a 1930 lecture, but was not published until 1943, whereas "Plato's Doctrine of Truth" had its source in a lecture course given at Freiburg in 1931–32, was composed in 1940, and first published in 1942. Some sources give 1930–31 as the date of the lecture course on Plato's allegory of the cave (e.g., *Wegmarken* [Frankfurt: Klostermann, 1967], p. 397, and *Wegmarken*, Gesamtausgabe Band 9 [Frankfurt: Klostermann, 1976], p. 483), but the later date is suggested both by the prospectus for the Heidegger Gesamtausgabe and the course list vetted by Heidegger himself, which appears in W. J. Richardson, *Heidegger: Through Phenomenology to Thought* (The Hague: Nijhoff, 1963), p. 667. This date is also the one given in *Wegmarken* 1976 on the contents page. The long period of gestation through which both essays passed means that when the original versions are eventually made available, they will provide a most valuable source for the study of the development of Heidegger's thinking on the history of Being.

4. "Kuria aletheian kai noun paraschomene" (*Republic* 517c). *Wegmarken* (1967), p. 136; trans. *Philosophy in the Twentieth Century*, 3:187.

5. *Parmenides*, Gesamtausgabe Band 34, hrsg. M. S. Frings (Frankfurt: Klostermann, 1982), p. 63 (lecture course given at Freiburg 1942–43).

6. M. Heidegger and E. Fink, *Heraklit* Seminar Wintersemester 1966/67 (Frankfurt: Klostermann, 1970), pp. 259–60; trans. C. H. Seibert, *Heraclitus Seminar 1966/67* (University, Ala.: University of Alabama Press, 1979), p. 161.

7. See for example: Henry G. Wolz, "Plato's Doctrine of Truth: Orthotes or Aletheia?", *Philosophy and Phenomenological Research* 27 (1966):157–82; S. Rosen, "Heidegger's Interpretation of Plato," *Journal of Existentialism* 7, no. 28 (1967):477–504; David A. White, "Truth and Being: A Critique of Heidegger on Plato," *Man and World* 7, no. 2 (1974):118–134; J. Phillippoussis, "Heidegger and Plato's Notion of Truth," *Dialogue* 15 (1976):502–4; William A. Galston, "Heidegger's Plato; A Critique of "Plato's Doctrine of Truth," *The Philosophical Forum* 13, no. 4 (1982):371–84; J. Grondin, "L' *aletheia* entre Platon et Heidegger," *Revue de Métaphysique et de Morale* 87, no. 4 (1982):551–56.

8. Paul Friedländer, *Platon*, Band 1, Zweite erweiterte und verbesserte Auflage (Berlin: Walter de Gruyter, 1954), pp. 233–42; *Plato* I An Introduction, trans. Hans Meyerhoff (New York: Pantheon, 1958), pp. 221–29; *Platon*, Band I, Dritte durchgesehene und ergänzte Auflage (Berlin: Walter de Gruyter, 1964), pp. 233–42; *Plato* I an Introduction, 2nd ed., trans. Hans Meyerhoff (Princeton: Princeton University Press, 1973). Christopher S. Nwodo has written a study of the Friedländer-Heidegger debate but he was apparently only aware of the first English version of Friedländer's study: "Friedländer versus Heidegger: *A-letheia* Controversy," *Journal of the British Society for Phenomenology* 10, no. 2 (1979):84–93.

9. *Platon* (1964), p. 242; *Plato* (1973), p. 229.

10. *Platon* (1964), p. 241; *Plato* (1973), p. 228.

11. H-G. Gadamer, "Plato und Heidegger," *Der Idealismus und seine Gegenwart*, Festschrift für Werner Marx zum 65. Geburtstag, hrsg. U. Guzzoni, B. Rang und L. Siep (Hamburg: Felix Meiner, 1976), p. 170; trans. I. Sprung, "Plato and Heidegger," *The Question of Being*, edited by M. Sprung (University Park, Pa.: Pennsylvania State University Press, 1978), p. 49.

12. The protocols of the seminars do not, of course, have the same textural authority as the texts Heidegger himself prepared for publication, but Heidegger himself cooperated when they were translated from French into German and the remark is somewhat emphatic: "Was hier gesagt ist, stimmt nicht; Parmenides sagt nichts Derartiges" (*Vier Seminare* p. 133).

13. On the notion of trace *(Spur)* in Heidegger, see J. Derrida, *Marges de la philosophie* (Paris: Minuit, 1972), p. 24–29; trans. A. Bass, *Margins of Philosophy* (Chicago: University of Chicago Press, and Brighton: Harvester, 1982), pp. 23–27.

14. This is an issue that Jacques Derrida especially has familiarized us with. See especially "Les fins de l'homme," *Marges*, pp. 162–64; trans. *Margins*, pp. 134–36.

15. "Has the 'not-yet-metaphysical' no reference at all to metaphysics? One could suppose the 'not-yet' to be cut off from what follows, from metaphysics. The 'not-yet' could, however, also be an 'already,' a certain preparation, which only we see as we do, and must see as we do, whereas Heraclitus could not see it," *Heraklit*, p. 123; trans. *Heraclitus Seminar 1966/67*, p. 75.

Chapter Three
"History is Seldom":
Hölderlin and Heidegger

1. The Dialogue betweeen Poet and Thinker

No one doubts the importance of Hölderlin's poetry for Heidegger's thinking, particularly after 1934, the time of the first lecture course on Hölderlin. The evidence is overwhelming. A number of the crucial words of Heidegger's later writings can readily be shown to have been drawn from Hölderlin's poems — words like *earth, the open, the holy, inwardness (Innigkeit), danger, the saving power (das Rettende), homecoming.* The notion of the fourfold of gods and mortals, heaven and earth, is rooted in Hölderlin. Even when Heidegger's mind seems firmly set on some other topic, it is quite common for a quotation from Hölderlin to be introduced. It might seem as if the only doubt is whether Hölderlin's influence should not be more readily apparent to us in writings before 1934. After all, we have Heidegger's own assurance that he felt the impact of Hölderlin much earlier. Referring to the publication of Hölderlin's Pindar translations in 1910 and of the late hymns in 1914, Heidegger says "these two books hit us students like an earthquake" (US 182; WL 78).

But the mapping of this influence throws very little light on its nature. Heidegger repeatedly asked about the nature of the relation of poet and thinker, so that we might have a better understanding of it than simply as a matter of "influence." For example, he says that "we may know something about the relation between philosophy and poetry, but we know nothing of the dialogue between poet and thinker, who" — and then he quotes Hölderlin —

dwell near to one another on mountains farthest apart.

(W 107; EB 392)

It is perhaps most like the dialogue between thinkers, of which Heidegger's *Kant and the Problem of Metaphysics* was an early example, and of which Heidegger repeatedly had to insist that it had its own rules. Certainly the dialogue between poet and thinker belongs neither to literary history, which considers such a dialogue a violation of what can be maintained on the basis of factual evidence, nor to philosophy, for which it is a random departure into fantasy. But then what does rule the dialogue? Heidegger's answer is that the dialogue is *seinsgeschichtlich*; it belongs to the history of Being. We are inclined to think of Heidegger's history of Being as a reworking of the history of philosophy according to the claim that the fundamental question of philosophy is the question of Being; but, of course, the sway of Being extends further than philosophy. The history of Being is a fate or destiny *(Geschick)*. Hence Heidegger's answer to the complaints of scholars and university philosophers is that "destiny pursues its course untroubled" (H 252; PLT 96). One understands by this that the dialogue between thinker and poet is not set up to order like a Philosophy and Literature Conference. Yet that still leaves us understanding very little about it.

The problem is that Heidegger's statements about "a secret kinship" *(eine verborgene Verwandtschaft)* between thinking and poetry have tended to serve more as slogans than as subjects for inquiry. We readily agree with him that both share a concern for language. There are numerous examples of Heidegger turning to poetry in his essays so that his reader can hear a long-forgotten word usage that he will revive or appeal to as evidence. Quite often it is Goethe to whom Heidegger turns, a fact worth noting in view of the legend that Heidegger despised Goethe. For Heidegger, this guardianship of language shared by poetry and thinking is no minor affair. Indeed this is how man serves as the shepherd of Being or corresponds to the destiny of Being (W 161–62; BW 210). Already in *Being and Time*, Heidegger had indicated that the business of philosophy was that of preserving "the force of the most elemental words" and that the failure to do so was a source of the pseudoproblems that occupied many philosophers (SZ 220; tr. 262). Examples Heidegger might have given are problems arising from the notion of an external world, the correspondence theory of truth or the subject-object distinction. The first step is always to dispel the self-evidence of these problems by claiming, on the basis of linguistic evidence, that far from being eternal questions, they are determined by historically bound presuppositions. But it must be recognized that this approach is only a tenuous stage preparatory to a complete rereading of the history of philosophy in terms of the history of Being, in which the traditional notion of philosophy is challenged.

The dialogue between poetry and thinking invites us therefore to look beyond the claim that the poet's task is, as T. S. Eliot has it, to "purify the dialect of the tribe."[1] Heidegger attempts to characterize the fundamental task of the language of poetry by introducing notions of an *Ursprache* or primal language (ED 40; EB 307) and of an *entwerfende Sagen* or "projective saying" (UK 84; PLT 74). These notions are to a limited extent similar to Merleau-Ponty's later notion of *parole parlante*, an originary speech that formulates for the first time. Certainly Heidegger recognizes — and this becomes especially clear in the essays on the poet Stefan George—that the special task of the poet is to put into language what has "never yet been spoken" (US 161;WL 59). But the historical dimension of language that is so central to Heidegger's conception is not developed in Merleau-Ponty. And it is the historical—in the sense of the history of Being—that is at the root of Heidegger's most important attempt to characterize the difference between poet and thinker. "The thinker says Being. The poet names the holy" (W 107; EB 391). These sentences do not provide us with a formula. We must not suppose that there is a technical difference between saying and naming, or that Being and the holy are different things.[2] The basis of the characterization is the fundamental similarity of poetry and thinking: "The like is like only as different."

What is at issue in this contrast between thinker and poet? Why does it appear, not when Heidegger is engaged in a dialogue with poetry, but in a postscript appended to the lecture "What is Metaphysics?", a lecture which was addressed not to poets but to the faculties of his university? This second question will be reserved for a later chapter when I shall take up that lecture and Heidegger's various "rereadings" of it. I shall approach the first question by way of an examination of Heidegger's essays on Hölderlin and in particular his reading of the poem *"Wie wenn am Feiertage...."* We shall have to recall Heidegger's best-known essay in the realm of art and literature, *The Origin of the Work of Art*. Only in the light of that essay can we avoid making of Heidegger's reading of Hölderlin a contribution to literary history or aesthetics. At the same time, *The Origin of the Work of Art* remains fundamentally incomplete without the essays on Hölderlin.

The Origin of the Work of Art belongs to the same period as the first lectures on Hölderlin and reflects a common concern. In the winter semester of 1934-35, Heidegger had taken as the text for his lecture course at Freiburg University, not a philosophical work but Hölderlin's two poems "Germanien" and "Der Rhein." Some of the material used in that course was subsequently reworked and incorporated into the 1936 Rome lecture "Hölderlin and the Essence of Poetry." Late in 1935, when *The Origin of the Work of Art* was delivered in its shorter version as a single lecture, Heidegger, in the company of the Rembrandt scholar Kurt Bauch, was giving a colloquium at Freiburg University under the title "The Overcoming of Aesthetics in the Question of Art." In 1936, with the addition, among other things, of the whole discussion of Van Gogh's painting of a pair of shoes, *The Origin of the Work of Art* was expanded to form three lectures. And the winter semester of 1936-37 saw the first of Heidegger's lecture courses devoted to Nietzsche, this one on the theme "The Will to Power as Art," and including discussions of Plato's treatment of art in relation to truth, Kant's *Critique of Judgement*, and a brief sketch of the history of aesthetics. We know nothing more than the title of the seminar with Bauch, and the first version of *The Origin of the Work of Art* remains unpublished. Nevertheless, even in the absence of that material, what emerges is a sustained attempt to confront the approach to art exhibited by "aesthetics." This confrontation with aesthetics provides us with a valuable model with which to approach the *Auseinandersetzung* with the whole history of Western philosophy in the changed form it took after the mid-1930s.

For Heidegger "aesthetics" is not the name of the autonomous discipline that arose in the eighteenth century once judgments of taste had come to be separated from the understanding and its concepts. This is how Gadamer interprets it in an introduction to Heidegger's *The Origin of the Work of Art*, which he provided when the essay was reprinted in 1960. In consequence, even though he recognized that Heidegger sought "to overcome the concept of aesthetics itself," Gadamer in fact understood that attempt to have only the same limited application that he referred to in *Truth and Method* when he identified as the subject of his own critique "the subjectivization of aesthetics."[3] But the first Nietzsche course, which gives us the best introduction to Heidegger's understanding of "aesthetics," specifically in its attempt to provide a brief history of aesthetics, insists that philosophical meditation on the essence of art and the beautiful had already begun as aesthetics in the age of Plato and Aristotle. Heidegger understands "aesthetics" to mean the consideration of man's state of feeling in relation to the beautiful. Whereas for Heidegger himself it is the *work of art* that is central, in aesthetics the artwork is represented as the bearer and instigator of the beautiful in relation to the state of feeling of either artist or observer (NI 92-94; Ni 78-79). In this way art is placed outside the truth.

Heidegger's right to use the term *aesthetics* to characterize the philosophical meditation on the essence of art as it takes place throughout the philosophical tradition is open to question and should be examined further. Heidegger and Gadamer might be expected to reach agreement on the claim that from the seventeenth century onward "meditation on the beautiful in art now slips markedly, even exclusively, into the relationship of man's state of feeling, *aisthesis*" (NI 99; Ni 83). What is at issue between them is not a matter that could be settled by historical investigations in any conventional sense. The point is rather that Heidegger's discussion of art and aesthetics is intimately tied to his attempt to overcome metaphysics, the history of Western ontology. Gadamer, by contrast, adopts a much more conciliatory attitude toward the tradition and particularly the Greeks, as may be illustrated by his rehabilitation of such concepts as *mimesis* and *ergon*.[4]

But what then does "the overcoming of aesthetics" amount to? How can it express itself if the whole tradition and all of its concepts are in question? It is important to understand that Heidegger's "historical" inquiry into aesthetics does not amount to isolating it in order to reject it. Rather "overcoming aesthetics," as it is practiced in the lecture series "Nietzsche: The Will to Power as Art" consists in finding exceptions to aesthetics, thinkers whose thought on art exceed aesthetics. So, giving Kant as his example, he concedes that "every true aesthetics explodes itself" (NI 154; Ni 131). This does not mean that Heidegger comes to read the *Critique of Judgment* as if it stood outside the Western philosophical tradition. The crux of the interpretation is in respect of the sentence, "Taste is the capacity to judge an object or mode of representation by means of delight or revulsion, devoid of all interest." Schopenhauer, and following him Nietzsche, understand the final phrase in the sense of "a pure repose." In Heidegger's rereading of Kant, the latter emerges as a thinker who reveals what aesthetics conceals—the way the beautiful, in the radiance of its coming to the fore, claims us (NI 130; Ni 110).

In the same way, Heidegger finds that it is Platonism and not Plato that effaces the discordance between beauty and truth. Nietzsche presents his thinking as an inverted Platonism. In consequence, when Nietzsche places art above truth, we must understand it as an inversion of the view, attributed to Plato, that truth is said to be higher than art. But for the most part, Plato's texts seem to maintain a distance between art and truth. In the *Phaedrus*, however, Heidegger finds a more salient passage, whereby beauty is accorded the role of being *ekphanestaton kai erasmiotaton* (Phaedrus 250d). Rejecting Ficino's translation of it in 1468 as *perspicua et amabilis* — "perspicuous and lovable" — Heidegger renders it *das Hervorscheinendste, aber auch das Entrückendste*, "the most radiant, but also the most enchanting."[5] The beautiful snatches us from the oblivion of Being and grants a view upon Being (NI 227-29; Ni 196-97). Plato himself and the Renaissance understanding of his text exhibit different conceptions of Being (NI 217; Ni 187). For Plato, the discordance between art and truth is a felicitous one, a severance that as an opening up of Being, is at bottom a concordance (NI 219-20; Ni 189). For Platonism, the discordance is effaced. For Nietzsche, the discordance arouses dread *(Entsetzen)*. In that way we find in the history of Plato's text the concealed history of the metaphysical tradition and its overcoming.

Again, although at an early stage of Heidegger's account he suggests that Nietzsche's meditation on art is not an inquiry into the work of art, further exploration convinces him that Nietzsche's notion of "form" serves as the title for the artwork in his thinking (NI 135 seq.; Ni 115 seq.). Similarly, although Nietzsche follows Schopenhauer's aesthetical reading of Kant's notion of disinterestedness, Nietzsche himself with the notion of "rapture" evades an aesthetical description of our relation to the artwork. So, according to Heidegger, Nietzsche's meditation on art also arrives at a peak that is no longer aesthetics (NI 161; Ni 137). Yet alongside this Nietzsche who is no longer tied to aesthetics, there nevertheless remains a Nietzsche who reads his predecessors so that they sustain aesthetics.

We can conclude then that the "overcoming of aesthetics" does not involve an elaborate exercise of setting up aesthetics so that it can be knocked down or put to one side. It amounts rather to turning the philosophical considerations of art toward a dialogue with the major thinkers of the tradition, a dialogue that takes up the central issues of the truth of the work of art. When Heidegger both disputes the reading of Western thought on art as aesthetics and at the same time declares that the philosophical meditation on art began as aesthetics, he is saying both that art is a destiny of the truth of Being and also that throughout this tradition, from the outset, that destiny is concealed. One of the ways in which the oblivion of Being takes place is as aesthetics. And the overcoming of aesthetics is to be accomplished by placing alongside the aesthetical, a conception that is no longer aesthetical and yet derives from the concealed destiny of the truth of Being as it comes—however partially—to be revealed. That it be so revealed is a precondition of Heidegger's capacity to interpret traditional writings on art in such a way that they are no longer confined to aesthetics.

From this brief discussion of the overcoming of aesthetics we shall carry forward three questions. First, why does Heidegger insist that philosophical meditation on the essence of art began as aesthetics? Second, what allows Heidegger to characterize the claim that "every true aesthetics explodes itself" as a historical fact? What allows him to say, in the same context, that aesthetics, while not accidental, is nevertheless also not what is essential? How are we supposed to understand the situation whereby the concealed destiny of the truth of Being comes to be revealed? What is Heidegger's account of that event? Third, why is the attempt to overcome aesthetics through a rereading of the major texts of traditional aesthetics not to be accomplished by a rewriting of the history of aesthetics so that in effect aesthetics itself disappears and passes into oblivion? Does not Heidegger seem to insist upon the need to maintain a memory of an "aesthetical" reading of these philosophical texts on art alongside his own "no longer aesthetical" reading? If we are not offered the two readings simply to point up Nietzsche's inadequacies as a reader or to emphasize Heidegger's own originality, what is the deeper necessity accompanying this task of rereading?

Toward the end of the lectures on Nietzsche and art, Heidegger remarks, "The more clearly and simply a decisive inquiry traces the history of Western thought back to its few essential stages, the more that history's power to reach forward, seize and commit grows. This is especially the case where it is a matter of overcoming such history" (NI 234; Ni 203). Heidegger finds the culmination of Nietzsche's own overturning of Platonism in the brief section of *Twilight of the Idols* entitled "How the 'True World' Finally Became a Fable: the History of an Error." Nietzsche offers in that place six divisions of the history of Platonism and there is a clear parallel between the six stages of Heidegger's history of the basic developments in aesthetics, except perhaps in their characterizations of the final phase: Nietzsche's account culminates in the declaration of the "end of the longest error" as part of a characterization of his own thinking and what it aspires to, whereas Heidegger does not include himself in his own account. Nevertheless a significant moment occurs for the charting of Heidegger's own self-understanding when, although only briefly, he emphasizes the importance of the death of God for Nietzsche's historical thinking and in particular for inspiring dread in the face of the discordance between art and truth (NI 251; Ni 217). As we shall see, the death of God – or, as it was thought by Hölderlin, "the default of God" – played a crucial role in the development of Heidegger's account of history.

2. The Work of Art and the Naming of the Holy

In the essay *The Origin of the Work of Art*, Heidegger makes his starting point the work of art and not the artist or the spectator. Both the creator and the preserver, which is his name for the observer who has put aside aesthetic connoisseurship, are subordinated to the work of art (UK 77; PLT 68). The essay studiously avoids reference to genius and maintains instead that art is itself an origin (UK 89; PLT 78). The work of art – and Heidegger specifically confines himself to great art (UK 39; PLT 40) – is originary in the sense of founding a world. He takes as his examples a temple and a sculpture of a god, both of which institute a world ruled by the divinities to which they are dedicated. This does not mean that the temple and the sculpture institute the divinities, but that a great work of art may serve as an origin by announcing and enshrining the truths of an epoch. The work of art is one of the sites where the decisions of history take place. To express it in a language Heidegger would reject for its subjectivist overtones, works of art found worldviews *(Weltanschauungen)*. In Heidegger's own words, the work of art is the origin of a people's historical existence *(Dasein)*; art is the setting to work of truth. The language of worldviews is inappropriate because we can choose between world-views, whereas each epoch and the works of art appropriate to it have a necessity of their own – a destiny (SD 62–63; TB 56). To free the concept of world from the neo-Kantian connotations of *Weltanschauung*, Heidegger introduces into his thinking the earth, which is the ground on which a historical people rests and yet which is not altogether within their purview.

Heidegger's *The Origin of the Work of Art* should thus be seen as an attempt to develop a vocabulary other than that of aesthetics with which to discuss art. The form-matter distinction, for example, gives way to the strife between world and earth and Heidegger clearly regards his sustained focus on the work of art as a point of difference between his own treatment and that of his predecessors (NI 138; Ni 118). But irrespective of the formal and historical difficulties it raises, any reading of *The Origin of the Work of Art* as an attempt to provide an alternative framework for the discussion of art will simply not do justice to Heidegger's text. The formal difficulty amounts to asking where one might hope to discover a language that did not have its sources in the language of the tradition. The historical difficulty would simply be a question of pointing out some of the sources of Heidegger's discussion both in the thinking of the Greeks and in German Idealism. Furthermore, it is not accidental that Heidegger takes as his major example a Greek temple. Heidegger, in his lectures on Nietzsche, associates the formation of a dominant aesthetics with the decline of great art (NI 95; Ni 80). He even claims, referring to the age of Plato and Aristotle, that "aesthetics begins with the Greeks only at that moment when their great art and also the great philosophy that flourished along with it comes to an end" (NI 95; Ni 80). This view is a consequence of his adoption not of an aesthetic criterion of great art, but of the almost Hegelian standard of "the way art shapes the history of an era—or remains irrelevant for it" (NI 94; Ni 79). Heidegger, far from insisting that art plays the decisive role in every epoch, as many readers of *The Origin of the Work of Art* have supposed, is in fact seeking to draw our attention to its failure to do that. The famous example of the Van Gogh painting of a pair of shoes was introduced, when the original 1935 version of the lecture was expanded to form three lectures, for the twofold purpose of elucidating the notions of equipmentality and of the truth of the thing. But the difference between Heidegger's account of the painting of a pair of shoes and his description of the temple has been insufficiently appreciated. Whereas the temple opens up a world, first giving to "things their look and to men their outlook on themselves" (UK 42-43; PLT 43), the painting of the peasant woman's shoes tells us no more than what the peasant woman knows without noticing or reflecting (UK 30; PLT 34). The difference helps clarify for us the way in which art is historical.

So the overcoming of aesthetics as it takes place in *The Origin of the Work of Art* is sought not in an attempt to find a different framework for the discussion of art, but in an account of the historical nature of art. To speak here of "the historical nature of art" means something very different from referring art to history as if in an attempt to explain it. Art itself is shown to be one of the ways in which history takes place. And history is neither the work of man, nor still less a straightforward chronology. History is understood as a rupture. It takes place in rare epoch-making events that determine what is and what is not; or as Heidegger puts it, recalling a fragment of Heraclitus (Diels 53), what is holy and what unholy, what great and what small, what brave and what cowardly, who master and who slave (UK 43; PLT 43). The historic is thought of as epochal, that is, in terms of the giving and withholding of Being.

Given his view of history, it is not surprising that when it comes to elucidating the essence of art as an origin Heidegger turns to the origins of Greek art. But the essay is as much about the end of art as its origin. This is somewhat obscured by the fact that the remarks about the so-called death of art are relegated to an epilogue in part written later. It is important to know that the original shorter version of the essay culminated in a discussion of Hegel. Many of the same issues that arise in the consideration of the relation between Hegel's history of philosophy and the account given by Heidegger are repeated (or one could even say that in certain respects are anticipated) in Heidegger's brief attempt to come to terms with Hegel's discussion of art. It might seem at first sight that Heidegger is simply raising the question as to whether Hegel's famous characterization about the past character of art is justified. In fact it seems that Heidegger accepts that insofar as art's basic task is that of "representing the absolute, i.e., of establishing the absolute definitively as such in the realm of historical man" (NI 100; Ni 84), the basic characterization is adequate. But just as aesthetics is for Hegel a history of worldviews that amounts to a history of truth, so for Heidegger the history of the nature of art is to be seen in relation to the history of the changes of the essence of truth (UK 94; PLT 81). And so the divergencies between Hegel's and Heidegger's accounts of art can now be seen to be in large measure governed by the question of the truth of the tradition and the conditions determining the emergence of that truth. We saw in the first chapter how that was a question of the different conceptions of the "end of philosophy" espoused by the two thinkers. So the question is repeated now in the realm of art as to whether Hegel's notion of the "end" is incomplete insofar as it does not ask in a sufficiently radical way about other possibilities. Restated, what is at issue is the relation between poetry and philosophy. Does poetry at its completion pass into philosophy, as Hegel would have it? Or should we not look to other possibilities of poetry as we must look for other possibilities of thinking than those offered by the philosophical tradition?

In the course of *The Origin of the Work of Art*, Heidegger accords poetry a privileged position. Poetry is for Heidegger the essence of art, and the essence of poetry is said to be the founding of truth (ED 38; EB 304). These remarks clearly point to the elucidation of *poiesis* as a fundamental word of Heidegger's thinking, especially in the essay *The Question concerning Technology*, which we shall turn to in chapter 5. Poetry in the narrow, more familiar sense is also given a privileged position among the arts and this because of the fundamental place of language.

The originary character of language, which is attested to by *The Origin of the Work of Art*, is elucidated in the essay *Hölderlin and the Essence of Poetry*. Heidegger says there that "the poet names the gods and names all things for what they are."[6] The parallel with the examples of the temple and the sculpture of the god is apparent. What Heidegger said of the temple in the essay on the work of art, that, in its standing there, it "first gives to things their look and to men their outlook on themselves" (UK 42-43; PLT 43), finds its parallel in the essay on Hölderlin. "When the gods are named originally and the essence of things finds its word, so that things first shine out, human existence *(Dasein)* is brought into a firm relation and set on a ground" (ED 39; EB 305). Heidegger refers to the closing words of the poem *Andenken*:

> Was bleibet aber, stiften die Dichter.

> But what endures, the poets establish.

Heidegger is referring here to the instituting of Being in language. The idea that Being is founded on the word of the poet is fundamental to all of Heidegger's thinking after this time, and the philosopher comes to be thought of in a similar light. Henceforth Being is always thought of in respect of its coming to language.

Nevertheless, the naming of the gods is not the same as the naming of the holy that Heidegger writes of when characterizing the difference between poet and thinker: "The thinker says Being; the poet names the holy." Until this is recognized, the full meaning of the characterization will remain unheeded. It is Heidegger's commentary on Hölderlin's poem *"Wie wenn am Feiertage..."* that explores the sense of the phrase "the poet names the holy."[7] In Hölderlin's poem we read the lines:

> Jetzt aber tagts! Ich harrt und sah es kommen,
> Und was ich sah, das Heilige sei mein Wort.

> But now day breaks! I waited in trust and saw it coming,
> And what I saw, may the holy be my word.

Heidegger delivered his commentary on this poem as a lecture in 1939 and 1940 and published it in 1941, which is also the time of the first sketches that we have of the history of Being. The poem presents numerous textual problems and Heidegger gives his own version of it, which his commentary is supposed to justify. Indeed the poem is clearly unfinished; for Heidegger this is a consequence of an excess *(Überfluss)* that may be referred to the holy.[8]

In Heidegger's reading, the poem hinges on the relation between the word *holy* and another crucial word in Hölderlin's poetry, *nature*. Heidegger states the relation as follows: "compelled, Hölderlin names nature 'the holy'" (ED 56). The word *nature*, Heidegger suggests, was no longer regarded as adequate (ED 54 and 67). It is overcome as the fundamental word of poetry by virtue of a primordially instigating saying (ED 57). We are thus witnessing the taking place of an overcoming. But that nature is overcome does not mean that it is a spent force.

> Die Natur ist jetzt mit Waffenklang erwacht,...

> Nature has now awoken with clamor of weapons,...

The weapons are those of the word. In the naming of the holy, nature wakes and unveils the holy as her essence. This points to an ambiguity, but it is not one that we can resolve by pointing to two senses of the word *nature*. The ambiguity belongs to the event. Looking back to the past, nature fulfills itself. Looking forward to the future, nature is found inadequate and is overcome.

Heidegger's elucidation of these terms is crucial. Nature is present *(west an)* in everything, in human work, and the fate of peoples. His account of nature in its relation to things suggests the ontological difference; in the word *nature* we can hear Being as it is understood in Heidegger's thinking before the mid-1930s. With the word *holy* Hölderlin names the open. The open is a notion of great importance for Heidegger's thinking: one of the ways in which he describes originary language, corresponding to Merleau-Ponty's *parole parlante*, is to say that it is that language that brings what is into the open.[9] Hölderlin's word *holy* not only illustrates originary language: it is a word that can be used to describe the work of originary language, including poetry.

How does the naming of the holy come about? To throw light on this, Heidegger introduces another text by Hölderlin, a commentary on a fragment by Pindar. It says in part, "The immediate, taken strictly, is impossible for mortals as for immortals. The law is strict mediacy." Heidegger understands the first of these sentences to say that the holy as immediate is inaccessible immediately to man and god. This provides an account of how the holy in the sense of the open has hitherto not been named, except mediately by naming the gods. As the naming of the gods is mediated, so the naming of the holy is impossible. For if naming is a mediation, how could the holy as immediate be mediated without destroying this immediacy? Heidegger's discussion of the way out of this dilemma is among the most difficult in all his works (ED 67).

The second sentence quoted from Hölderlin's commentary on Pindar, "the law is strict mediacy," provides the clue. The holy is immediate in the sense that it does not arise from mediation. In respect of the relation between gods and men, which both belong to the holy, the holy is strict mediacy (ED 67). The holy is both, on the one hand, the immediate, chaos, and on the other, it is mediacy, law.[10] The immediate maintains itself in this mediacy without being reduced to something mediated when the holy gives itself in the word (ED 70). The important point here is that the donation of the word *holy* is not the work of the poet, which would indeed be a mediation, but is itself—borrowing a word from Hölderlin's *Am Quell der Donau*—"by the holy compelled" *(heiliggenöthiget)* (ED 56 and 187 seq.).

We can best elucidate what has been accomplished by this essay on Hölderlin's *"Wie wenn am Feiertage..."* by placing it alongside *The Origin of the Work of Art*. The sense of "origin" has been clarified. We can now speak not only of art, but also the naming of the gods, as origins. And Heidegger understands the fundamental words of a thinker, the "words of Being," in the same way. The words for Being are titles for the rule that holds sway in different historical epochs. These epochs are not to be understood as historical periods. They must be understood in terms of the granting and withholding of Being, the granting of Being through the rule of the word that determines how things are and how they are not. The words for Being are not just formal titles or description that might be provided afterward. They are, like the work of art in Heidegger's understanding of it, originary.

Equally the role of the poet is clarified. This is important because it has sometimes been objected that Heidegger attempts to overcome the aesthetics of genius simply by saying very little about the creator. Furthermore, we shall find that having elucidated the place of the poet, Heidegger also deepened his understanding of the place of the thinker. Heidegger emphasizes the silence, the stillness, of the poet in waiting (ED 65). He clarifies it in respect of these lines from the poem:

> Und wie im Aug' ein Feuer dem Manne glänzt,
> Wenn hohes er entwarf, so ist
> Von neuem an den Zeichen, den Thaten der Welt jezt
> Ein Feuer angezündet in Seelen der Dichter.

> And as a fire gleams in the eye of that man,
> When he projects high things, so
> Anew in the signs, in the deeds of the world,
> A fire is now kindled in the souls of the poets.

Heidegger's comments, "As the high project of the reflective man is reflected in his gaze, so something light beams forth in the souls of the poets, when the holy unveils itself in coming" (ED 62). The crucial word here is *project (Entwurf)*. In *Being and Time*, the project belongs within the circularity of the worldhood of the world, whereby that wherein *(Worin)* human being *(Dasein)* lives is that upon which *(Woraufhin)* beings are discovered (SZ 86; tr. 119). The project as the disclosure of that for which Dasein exists, its possibilities, gives to things their aspect and is thus reflected in them. In *The Origin of the Work of Art* this perspective is already overcome. It is the poem as origin that gives things their aspect and men their outlook on themselves. The projective saying is not the project of a poet. The holy donates the originary word to the poet who reflects it.

This insight serves as the culmination of the essay and is its contribution to the overcoming of aesthetics. Heidegger points to the word *Hymnos* as Hölderlin's word. This does not mean that Heidegger has put the word *holy* to one side. *Hymnos* is the word of the holy in the sense that the hymn is not a hymn to nature, but a hymn of the holy (ED 76).

Und was ich sah, das Heilige sei mein Wort.

And what I saw, may the holy be my word.

The last phrase is in the optative mood to reflect that it is primarily the holy that donates the word.[11] The poet, struck by the holy, enters into its embrace. He quakes from remembrance *(Erinnerung)* of the destiny of Semele in her embrace with a god. The poet prays that his destiny is to say the holy rather than to suffer, as did Semele (ED 67-68).

3. The Default of God and Another Beginning

Standing on its own, Heidegger's essay *"Wie wenn am Feiertage..."* remains fundamentally obscure. The essay is concerned with the naming of the holy, but it does not seek to clarify why this should be the time of the donation of the holy:

But now day breaks!

In what sense should this "now" be understood? The essay allows a great deal of the essential background to remain implicit and particularly striking is the absence of any development of the idea of the "default of God" *(der Fehl des Gottes)*. The explication of this phrase is a crucial component of Heidegger's understanding of Hölderlin elsewhere. For example, the 1946 essay commemorating Rilke, "What Are Poets For?", draws our attention to the seventh stanza of the poem *Brot und Wein*. It begins:

Aber Freund! wir kommen zu spät. Zwar leben die Götter,
Aber über dem Haupt droben in anderer Welt.

But, my friend, we come too late. The gods are alive,
But above our heads, up there in another world.

The final lines of the stanza run:

So zu harren, und was zu tun indes und zu sagen,
Weiss ich nicht, und wozu Dichter in dürftiger Zeit?
Aber sie sind, sagst du, wie des Weingotts heilige Priester,
Welche von Lande zu Land zogen in heiliger Nacht.

> Always waiting, and what to do and say,
>   I do not know, and what are poets for in unpropitious times?
> But they are, you say, like the holy priests of the winegod,
>   Who travelled from land to land in holy night.

Heidegger explicitly relates the poet's saying of the holy to the default of the gods or of God. "To be a poet in an unpropitious time means: to attend, singing, to the trace of the fugitive gods. That is why the poet in the time of the world's night says the holy" (H 251; PLT 94). It is because "holy names are lacking" that Hölderlin can name the holy. The lack of holy names—the phrase is drawn from the poem *Heimkunft / An die Verwandten*—arises because the gods have fled. The complete sentence runs:

> Schweigen müssen wir oft; es fehlen heilige Nahmen,
> Herzen schlagen und doch bleibet die Rede zurück?

> Often we must keep silence; holy names are lacking,
> Hearts beat and yet does speech hold back?

It is in the silence arising from the lack of holy names that the open to which gods and men belong announces itself. "The holy" is the poet's name for the open. Hence the "holy night" of the god's default is also the dawn in which the holy comes to language in the hymns. The word *nature*, as noted earlier, looks both backward and forward. The default of the gods is not a straightforward absence but a shortcoming.[12]

We are now in a position to understand better what Heidegger means when he says of the dialogue between thinker and poet that it is a matter of the history of Being. Although Heidegger does not, in his essay on the poem "*Wie wenn am Feiertage...*," refer explicitly to the history of Being or the destiny of the truth of Being, it is to this essay that he points his readers when in the *Letter on Humanism* he introduces these notions (W 166 n; BW 215 n). The reference can only be explained on the grounds that Heidegger gains an essential insight into the history of Being in the dialogue with Hölderlin. This is not to say that Heidegger takes the idea over from Hölderlin. That would be a matter of influence, a term that is no longer appropriate here, because it fails to capture the sense in which this is truly a dialogue.

It is a dialogue in the sense Merleau-Ponty elucidates when he introduces us to the order of "instructive spontaneity," where one can no longer tell what came from my partner and what was my own contribution.[13] Just as Heidegger the thinker won his insight into the history of Being from the dialogue, so it is only the thinker who has already posed the question of Being who can recognize the naming of the holy as arising from historical destiny. "The holy, which alone

is the essential sphere of divinity, which in turn alone affords a dimension for
the gods and for God, comes to radiate only when Being itself beforehand and
after extensive preparation has been illuminated and is experienced in its truth"
(W 169; BW 218). That is why we must resist the temptation to distinguish what
modern scholarship finds in Hölderlin from what Heidegger finds there by identifying any addition to the former as Heidegger's addition. The essays on
Hölderlin are not simply vehicles for Heidegger's philosophy; Heidegger genu-
inely learns as he reads Hölderlin. A dialogue has a spirit of its own that cannot
be reduced to the sum of its partners.

But what is the insight into the essence of thinking that arises out of what the
poet says poetically about the essence of poetry? We must recall that when
Heidegger, at the beginning of *Being and Time*, posed anew the forgotten
question of Being, it seemed as if he was simply reviving the ancient questions
of Plato and Aristotle. It seemed that, in proposing the task of "a destruction of
the history of ontology," Heidegger merely sought to eliminate that sediment
that blocks our access to the "primordial experiences" underlying the tradition
(SZ 22; tr. 44). What might be meant by a "primordial experience," what our
access might be to such primordial sources, was far from clear in *Being and
Time*. The appeal to such experiences gives way in Heidegger's later writings to
the notion of "trace" *(Spur)*, as already referred to above in the discussion of
a-letheia. The "trace" arises not only in Heidegger's discussion of Anaximander,
but also in that of Hölderlin, where it is the task of the poet in destitute times
"to attend, singing, to the trace of the fugitive gods" (H 251; PLT 94). The
notion of trace addresses the issue of the concealment of presence, its absence,
in a way that was lacking in Heidegger's early formulations. Above all it helped
Heidegger to pass beyond the experience of absence in "the age for which the
ground fails to come" to an anticipation based on remembrance. The poet, like
the phenomenologist in Heidegger's conception, is a student of the inconspicu-
ous and the hidden.

Hölderlin, like Heidegger, experienced the fact that poet and thinker could no
longer perform their ancient roles. The thinker maintains him- or herself in
questioning, just as the poet waits for the gods. Hölderlin found that the gods
had fled and could no longer be named, and when Heidegger came to reflect
further on the peculiar lack of perplexity of the thinker when he or she
confronts the question of Being, he recognized a parallel between poet and
thinker. Through the lack of a word of Being, Being—in the sense of the history
of Being—came to light. The withholding of a word for Being disclosed the fact
that Being had not been recognized in those words that distilled a thinker's
deepest thoughts and served, as was said of the work of art, to announce and
enshrine the ultimate truth of an epoch. Those words of Being were at once a
giving and withholding of Being, *disclosing Being, but not disclosing themselves
as doing so.*

In this way, the history of philosophy emerged as the history of the naming of Being, or, as Heidegger would tend to call it more simply, "the history of Being." Notwithstanding the fact that Heidegger retained his conviction in the power of origins, the notion of the history of Being lent a greater dignity to those thinkers who stand between us and the Greeks. They could not be viewed as links in a chain or even conspirators in an ever-growing oblivion of Being. They too were beneficiaries of the dispensation of Being as it took place through the transformations of the essence of truth. The notion of "words for Being," or better "words *of* Being" insofar as it conveys that it is Being itself that speaks in the word, is an essential component of the idea of a history of Being. Heidegger's recognition and understanding of the history of Being owes a clear debt to his reading of Hölderlin and his confrontation with the problem of the historical nature of art more generally.

If we now return to Heidegger's phrase, "The poet names the holy," we find it should be understood in not one but two different senses. First of all, each poet names the holy insofar as he names the gods who belong with the mortals in the open of the holy. More fundamentally, this insight into the essence of poetry as the naming of the gods and of all things as what they are, arises at the time of the default of the gods. This default allows the poet of that time to name the holy itself. Hölderlin is that poet and because of his insight into the essence of poetry, Heidegger calls him the poet of poets (ED 32; EB 295).

"The thinker says Being" also bears a twofold sense. Corresponding to the poet naming the gods, each thinker names Being, although he is unaware that this is his task as a thinker. Only the thinker at the time of the withholding of a name for Being has the decisive insight into the history of Being and hence into the thinker's vocation. As that thinker, Heidegger would be a candidate for the title of "thinker of thinkers" in parallel with the title he gives Hölderlin, were it not for his own insistence that his thinking is merely provisional.

When the poet names the gods of the thinker within the tradition, he or she gives to that tradition a fundamental word; there is an instituting, in the sense described in *The Origin of the Work of Art*. One sense or mode of this instituting is, as mentioned earlier, that of a bestowal or excess (UK 88; PLT 77). This excess breaks through the continuity of sequential history as ordinarily conceived, and forms a beginning. Heidegger is referring to this excess when he says at the end of his essay on "*Wie wenn am Feiertage...*": "History is seldom." Heidegger's own elucidation runs, "History is there only when the essence of truth is originally decided" (ED 73).

The phrase "History is seldom" has a still more rarefied sense in respect to the naming of the holy by the poet of poets and the saying of Being by the thinker of thinkers. According to this view of history, Hölderlin and Heidegger share the same time, even though almost one hundred and twenty years lie between their births. This is because they both belong to the epoch of the withdrawal of Being, and recognize it not only as an end, a closure, but also as an opening, another beginning, another history. They stand in a between-time. This is what it means to say that the holy night is also a dawn:

But now day breaks!

The experience of the flight of the gods already points to the coming of the gods.[14] The experience of the end of philosophy already announces another way of thinking. Heidegger proceeds with this question of "another beginning" by recalling the beginning of the metaphysical tradition. The "first beginning" is not left behind. The tradition is overcome only through its remembrance. That is why it is called "another beginning" and not simply "a new beginning."[15]

This may be illustrated from Heidegger's essay *"Wie wenn am Feiertage...."* For all Hölderlin's remarkable insight, both into the Greeks and into his own time, he did not, according to Heidegger, recognize the import of the word *physis*, although *nature* made an appearance in the poem. "Nature" is the usual translation of *physis*. For Heidegger it means "the self-opening which opening out at the same time returns into that emergence" (ED 55). According to Heidegger, the word *nature* in Hölderlin's poem speaks according to its concealed truth. That is to say, the thinker offers a reading of *nature* in the poem, in which the heritage of this word, which passed from Heraclitus on through all of Western philosophy, resounds. But all of this goes unnoticed by Hölderlin himself. The oblivion of the destiny of Being in art is such, so Heidegger claims, that Hölderlin, for all his insight into the essence of poetry and his reputation as one of the most philosophical of poets, fails to see how the word relates to the essence of thinking. Whereas Heidegger recalls the founding word of Western thinking, Hölderlin's remembrance is of Semele. The name "Semele" arises in a discourse that still recalls the relation of humanity with its gods; Heidegger, by contrast, recalls one of the founding words in which the thinkers of Greece said Being.

But Heidegger's characterization of thinker and poet must not be read as an attempt to define or limit their respective roles. When Heidegger writes that "the thinker says Being, the poet names the holy," he speaks out of the experience of the oblivion of Being and in particular the growing oblivion of the destiny of Being in art as it takes place in aesthetics. This experience already points beyond itself so that the very distinction between poet and thinker must be placed in question. If the essence of poetry is to be decided anew by the "future poets" (ED 69), the same must be true of the essence of thinking. Today we are compelled by a necessity that dictates that we still need the terms *poet* and *thinker*, whether we are looking back to characterize the "poetic thinking" of the "first beginning" or turned forward to the future and whatever it might bring. And yet Heidegger has so little offered us definitions of the terms *poet* and *thinker* that, on the contrary, we are released from all attempts to delimit their essence. "Hölderlin writes poetry about the essence of poetry — but not in the sense of a timelessly valid concept. This essence of poetry belongs to a determinate time. But not in such a way that it merely conforms to this time, as to one which is already in existence. It is that Hölderlin, in the act of establishing the essence of poetry, first determines a new time" (ED 44; EB 313). Similarly, Heidegger writes about both the thinker and the poet from remembrance of the thinker of metaphysics and the poet of aesthetics. But in so doing he ceases to write of them only. The ability to say what metaphysics is, is granted only to those who are no longer bound by metaphysics in the sense of being within it; they can say only what it no longer is. Similarly, when it is said who the poet and thinker are, to be a poet or thinker becomes something different. To say who poet and thinker are in terms of aesthetics and metaphysics respectively, and at the same time to show the inner unity of aesthetics and metaphysics, is to present the conditions for a radical questioning of the very distinction between poet and thinker, a questioning that has its source in the dialogue between them.

In the context of a discussion of the oldest fragment of Western thinking, the Anaximander fragment, Heidegger emphasizes the sense in which poetry and thinking belong together. All poetry, both in the broad and the narrow sense, is a thinking; and thinking, which pronounces what the truth of Being dictates, is poetry (H 303; EGT 19). The radical questioning of the difference between poet and thinker as they exist in metaphysics, is already inscribed within remembrance of the origins of Greek thinking. The trace of that inscription still guides us when we seek a language for thinking that will not be bound by the language of metaphysics.

NOTES

1. T. S. Eliot, "Little Gidding," *Collected Poems 1909-1962* (London: Faber, 1963), p. 218.

2. Heidegger is not here making a distinction between "saying" and "naming." Heidegger on occasion writes of poetry as "the naming of Being" (*Erläuterungen zu Hölderlins Dichtung*, p. 40; trans. *Existence and Being*, p. 307). And he also says that the poet "says" the holy (*Holzwege*, p. 251; trans. *Poetry, Language, Thought*, p. 94).

3. H-G. Gadamer, "Einleitung," *Der Ursprung des Kunstwerkes*, p. 110; trans. D. E. Linge, *Philosophical Hermeneutics* (Berkeley: University of California Press, 1976), p. 218. *Wahrheit und Methode*, 3 Auflage (Tubingen: J. C. B. Mohr, 1972), pp. 39 seq.; trans. W. Glen-Doepel, *Truth and Method* (London: Sheed & Ward, 1975), pp. 39 seq.

4. *Wahrheit und Methode*, pp. 105-15; *Truth and Method*, pp. 99-108.

5. *Platonis Opera*, tralatione Marsilii Ficini, Basileae in officina Frobeniana, 1532, p. 452.

6. *Erläuterungen zu Hölderlins Dichtung*, p. 38; trans. *Existence and Being*, p. 304. The phrase "the naming of the gods" does not refer to the gods only, but to the nominating

of all things to their Being. At the same time, it should be said that the gods are not simply one more thing to be named, but are, as we shall see, essential to naming as such.

7. The essay can be found in *Erläuterungen zu Hölderlins Dichtung*, zweite Auflage, pp. 47-74. I have had the benefit of an unpublished translation made by John Raffan during 1975-76. During that time we – together with David Pollard – discussed the essay frequently and I remember those conversations with gratitude. When translating the poem, I have consulted the translations by Hamburger in *Friedrich Hölderlin, Poems and Extracts* (London: Routledge & Kegan Paul, 1966), pp. 373-77. On the textual problems raised by the poem, see W. A. O'Brien, "Getting Blasted: Hölderlin's 'Wie wenn am Feiertage...,'" *MLN* 94 (April 1979):569-86.

8. *Erläuterungen zu Hölderlins Dichtung*, pp. 73 and 125. Excess *(Überfluss)* in Heidegger refers to a historical founding. *Der Ursprung des Kunstwerkes*, p. 86; trans. *Poetry, Language, Thought*, p. 75.

9. *Erläuterungen zu Hölderlins Dichtung*, p. 57. Also *Erläuterungen zu Hölderlins Dichtung*, p. 40; trans. *Existence and Being*, p. 307. M. Merleau-Ponty, *Phénoménologie de la perception* (Paris: Gallimard, 1945), pp. 207 n and 229; trans. C. Smith, *Phenomenology of Perception* (London: Routledge & Kegan Paul, 1970), p. 178 n and 197.

10. On chaos and law see also *Nietzsche I*, p. 151; trans. *Nietzsche 1: The Will to Power as Art*, p. 128.

11. Cf. Paul de Man, "Les exégèses de Hölderlin par Martin Heidegger" *Critique* 11-13 (1955), p. 812; trans. *Blindness and Insight*, second edition (Minneapolis: University of Minnesota Press and London: Methuen, 1983), p. 258. This interpretation is corrected by Michael Murray "Heidegger and Hölderlin" *The Eighteenth Century* 21 (1980), p. 47.

12. *Hölderlins Hymnen 'Germanien' und der 'Rhein'*, Gesamtausgabe Band 39 (Frankfurt: Klostermann, 1980), pp. 229-38. Also Ruth-Eva Schulz-Seitz, "'Bevestigter Gesang' Bemerkungen zu Heideggers Hölderlin-Auslegung," *Durchblicke*, hrsg. V. Klostermann (Frankfurt: Klostermann, 1970), pp. 78-81.

13. *La Prose du Monde* (Paris: Gallimard, 1969), p. 28; trans. J. O'Neill, *The Prose of the World* (Evanston, Ill.: Northwestern University Press, 1973, and London: Heinemann, 1974), p. 19. *Signes* (Paris: Gallimard, 1960), p. 121; trans, R. C. McClary, *Signs* (Evanston, Ill.: Northwestern University Press, 1969), p. 97

14. "Das Gedicht," *Erläuterungen zu Hölderlins Dichtung*, pp. 182-92. According to Pöggeler, the coming gods are discussed by Heidegger in the unpublished *Beiträge zur Philosophie* dating from 1936-38: O. Pöggeler, "Heideggers 'Begegnung mit Hölderlin'" *Man and World* 10, no. 1 (1977):38.

15. See chapter 6, note 15.

Chapter Four
"Where the word is wanting...":
George and Heidegger

1. George's Poem *Das Wort*: Two Views of Language

Being and Time opens by reminding us that the question of Being has been forgotten. The book suffered for many years from being misread as an anthropological treatise. That was why it was still necessary some thirty-five years after its initial publication for Heidegger to insist to his readers that the fundamental experience underlying *Being and Time* is that of the oblivion of Being (SD 31; TB 29). In the 1930s and early 1940s, in his reading of Hölderlin, Heidegger explored the conditions for remembering the question of Being, as a question that had been forgotten. At the same time he explored the relation between the thinker who remembered this question and previous thinkers, both those like Aristotle who, it seemed, had asked the question and those like Descartes who, according to the Heidegger of *Being and Time*, had failed to raise the question. It was clear that in remembering the question of Being, the question was not simply undergoing a revival. In "raising again" *(Wiederholen)* that question, Heidegger was engaging in the "gathering" *(Versammeln)* that takes place at the "end" of philosophy.[1] Heidegger's notion of the history of Being arises as a development of the repetition of the question of Being.

The "dialogue" with Hölderlin, in which Heidegger clarifies the relation between the thinker and Being, had already focused on language. But it was in lectures on another poet, Stefan George, that Heidegger was able to identify with a special clarity the sense in which the experience of his thinking was an experience undergone with language, one that not only necessitated a transformed relation to language simply to express it, but also of its own accord transformed our relation to language. Between the end of 1957 and the beginning of 1959, Heidegger gave two separate lectures and one lecture series on language. The three-part lecture series, "The Essence of Language," and the lecture "The Word," both take as their starting point a poem by Stefan George, *Das Wort*.[2] Although there are at times slight differences of emphasis between the two essays, they are of no importance for the present purpose and I shall consider them together. The poem itself was first published in *Blätter fur die Kunst XI/XII* (1919) and was reprinted in *Das Neue Reich* (1928) in a section entitled *Das Lied* or "Song."

Das Wort

Wunder von ferne oder traum
Bracht ich an meines landes saum

Und harrte bis die graue norn
Den namen fand in ihrem born —

Drauf konnt ichs greifen dicht und stark
Nun blüht und glänzt es durch die mark...

Einst langt ich an nach guter fahrt
Mit einem kleinod reich und zart

Sie suchte lang und gab mir kund:
"So schläft hier nichts auf tiefem grund"

Worauf es meiner hand entrann
Und nie mein land den schatz gewann...

So lernt ich traurig den verzicht:
Kein ding sei wo das wort gebricht.

The Word

Wonder from afar or dream
I brought to the border of my land

And tarried until the grey norn
Found the name in her bourn —

Thereupon I could grasp it tight and strong
Now it blossoms and gleams throughout the mark...

Once I arrived after a good journey
With a gem rich and frail

She sought long and gave me to know:
"Nothing sleeps here above deep ground"

Whereupon it escaped my hand
And my land never attained the treasure...

So sadly I learned renunciation:
Where the word is wanting no thing can be.[3]

In Heidegger's reading, the poem is not about a poet who just happens to be having difficulty writing, a poet who is going through a bad patch. The poem describes an experience that the poet undergoes with language in which his relation to language is transformed. The first three stanzas describe the poet's previous relation to language, which seems to correspond to an instrumentalist view of language. With the word, the poet grasps something that is known by him independently and prior to language.[4] Language enables the poet to represent *(darstellen)* what is already known to presentifying thinking *(Vorstellen)*. We are also given an indication of how the poet previously conceived poetry; poetry *(Dichtung)* was a tight unyielding grasp *(greifen dicht und stark)*. Heidegger also introduces in his discussion here the notion of beauty, but it is not that the words are beautiful, rather that the things, poetic things—wonders and dreams—are made beautiful through poetic language.

This view of language is disturbed by an experience in which the poet, failing to discover an appropriate word for what he has in hand, finds that what he ought to name fades away. The poet thereby gains an insight both into the relation between word and thing and that between word and poet. First, he learns that without the word the thing cannot be retained. This corresponds to an account of language Heidegger had presented in essays from the mid-1930s onward. For example, in *The Origin of the Work of Art* he had written that "language, by naming beings for the first time, first brings beings to word and to appearance" (UK 84; PLT 73). It would seem that the poet comes to learn that language is an origin and thereby gains insight into what he elsewhere calls the "essence of poetry." In Hölderlin's words, often quoted by Heidegger:

> Was bleibet aber, stiften die Dichter.

> But what endures, the poets establish.

This does not mean that the poet has it in his or her power to establish something. At the end of the poem, George sorrowfully learns renunciation. Quite clearly he does not renounce what is said in the last verse of the poem:

> Where the word is wanting no thing may be.

The last verse serves to help us understand the new relation to language learned by the poet. The poet renounces his former view of the relation between word and thing. But not only that. He also renounces having words under his control. There is again a clear parallel between what George learns and Heidegger's own view. That we do not possess control over language is said most potently in the 1950 essay entitled "Language" in the phrase *Die Sprache spricht*, "Language speaks." It is not so much that man speaks, but that man speaks only insofar he responds to language (US 20; PLT 197).

Language speaks wherever and whenever human beings speak. In order to provide a phenomenological basis for this claim, Professor Volkmann-Schluck has drawn attention to the familiar phenomenon of being unable to force the right word to come to us: we silence ourselves and listen to the silence. Sometimes language speaks out of that silence and gives us what we were looking for. Professor Volkmann-Schluck comments on the statement "language speaks": "This sentence of Heidegger's does not promulgate some mystic profundity concerning language....But it expresses a simple, as well as enigmatical matter."[5] What he fails to acknowledge is that Heidegger himself had given the case of failing to find the right word for something as an example of language speaking as language. But Heidegger had then swiftly passed on to the instance of poetry, where something that has never yet been spoken is brought to language (US 161–62; OWL 59). Language speaks first and foremost in originary speaking, in poetry. One might restate the movement of the poem *Das Wort* as that of a passage from the paradigm of "the right word" for something toward a deeper understanding of poetic saying. This would not be to dismiss the experience of finding the right word for something. Such an experience does take place. But, to appeal to a distinction made by Heidegger elsewhere, it is an experience undergone with a given, actual language *(die jeweilige Sprache)* and not with the projective saying *(das entwerfende Sagen)*, that "brings the unsayable into the world" (UK 84; PLT 74).

It might be objected that the poem has not so far been treated as poetry. It seems rather to have been the excuse for a confrontation with the philosophy of language, and one might at this stage suppose that the poem was selected only to provide an occasion for Heidegger to rehearse his view of language. But if Heidegger begins both his lectures on the poems by drawing attention to parallels between what the poem appears to say and his own position, this is only meant to be the first step in his reading. The essays on George are as much a "dialogue between poet and thinker" as were the essays on Hölderlin. And they warrant the title "dialogue" only insofar as the reading is not a one-sided projection of an already established position. The thinker learns from the poet and at the same time the poet, by being heard, comes into his own. This means that something takes place in the reading. It is a different matter indeed from translating a poem into philosophical language or showing a poem's roots in a specific philosophy.

The original title of the lecture that we now know under the title "The Word" was *Dichten und Denken*, "Poetry and Thinking." The lecture exhibits the proximity of poetry and thinking by entering into the realm where poet and thinker are bound to each other. This is what "relation" *(Verhältnis)* comes to mean in Heidegger: a being held. But here poet and thinker are neighbors, not only in the event of the so-called dialogue, but also by virtue of the theme of the poem, the relation between word and thing. The dialogue between poet and thinker here arises out of a resemblance between their fundamental experiences with word and thing.

And yet there is a difficulty in identifying the poet's experience. Because the prize spoken of in the poem remains nameless, it might seem that we will never know what the poet had in hand. In that case the poet's experience would remain mysterious. Does the poem then give no hint about the treasure that evaded the poet's grasp? Heidegger claims that there is such a hint. In "The Essence of Language" Heidegger approaches the poet's experience only by way of a discussion of the corresponding experience of the thinker, but in the essay "The Word" he proceeds through an interpretation of the poet's renunciation to the conclusion that the treasure that never graced the poet's land is the word for the word (US 236; WL 154). The renunciation that the poet learns arises from his entrance into the realm of the unsayable. The source is silent. It denies his request for a word for the treasure. Nevertheless the poet is not silent in consequence. He still writes the poem and in it he tells us that he learned something from what had happened. He did not learn *about* language; the poet is not a philosopher of language. He learns to speak differently. The title of this different way with language is "renunciation." Renouncing is not something negative. It is a way of retaining the treasure in commemorative thinking *(Andenken)*.

But how can the poet retain something when he lacks the word for it? Did not the final verse make clear that where there was no word, there could be no thing? The thing could not be held, retained. But what if the poet's treasure was not a *thing* at all? Then presumably the dictum would not apply. But if it does not apply, why does it stand at the end of the poem?

According to Heidegger, the poet's treasure is indeed no thing. It is the word as word (US 191-93; WL 86-87). What George was seeking could well have been the word for the word, if the final verse

Where the word is wanting no thing can be

may be understood as consistent with this interpretation. This is the point where the thinker may claim to bring the poet into his own, that is, may claim to hear anew what the poem says. The underlying experience of the poem *Das Wort* is, on Heidegger's reading of it, not simply that of the lack of the word, but that of the lack of the word for the word. In the language of thinking, "the word for the word" means "the name for the Being of language."

2. The Thinker's Experience and the Question of Metaphysics

The experience of the lack of a word for Being underlies Heidegger's essay "What is Metaphysics?" and becomes thematic in the introduction and post-script subsequently added to it. The essay was originally Heidegger's inaugural lecture as Professor at Freiburg University, delivered in July 1929. The post-script, which included the sentences "The poet names the holy. The thinker says Being," which provided the focal point of the previous chapter, was added to the fourth edition of 1943. And an introduction, almost as long as the original lecture, was added to the fifth edition of 1949. In other words, these texts predate the essays on George by some years and we should therefore not be surprised if we occasionally find differences between them. Nevertheless, in spite of any such differences, the essays on George may be seen as part of Heidegger's continuing reflection on the themes of his inaugural lecture. We must in consequence pause in our examination of Heidegger's reading of George's poem to recall Heidegger's "What is Metaphysics?" and his own attempts to "reread" it in the light of his ever-deepening appreciation of the experience underlying his thinking.

The lecture "What is Metaphysics?" is largely concerned with the experience of the nothing, and Heidegger offers his reader the mood of anxiety or dread *(Angst)* as an entry point to it; "Anxiety reveals the nothing" (W 9; BW 103). Anxiety is distinguished from fear. Whereas fear is always of something determinate that threatens us, the indeterminacy of that before which we feel anxious is fundamental to Heidegger's characterization of anxiety. Heidegger writes of anxiety that in it "all things and we ourselves sink into indifference." Over twenty years later he provided a gloss that reads: "Beings no longer address *(ansprechen)* us."[6] They no longer speak to us, but yet, in our failure to get a hold on them, they come to oppress us. A few lines later in the lecture, Heidegger adds that anxiety deprives us of speech: *Die Angst verschlägt uns das Wort.* So that we find here the conjunction, familiar from George's poem, of the loss of words and of things.

Heidegger's attempt to elucidate this conjunction in the course of the lecture can be found in an important sentence to which we shall have to return later for what it says about language. "Because beings as a whole slip away, so that just the nothing crowds round, in the face of anxiety all utterance of the 'is' falls silent." For the moment, the important point being made here is that the nothing does not arise out of beings as a whole; it is always already there, though concealed. Proof of the "presence" of the nothing is found in the compulsive chatter that attempts to shatter the silence.[7] The nothing can be recognized in our preoccupation with beings. That we turn to beings in an attempt to escape the nothing, means that the nothing directs us to beings. The nothing is revealed as already there by our attempts to avoid it.[8]

At this point we must remember that in reading this lecture we miss every-thing if we take as our starting point what Heidegger says *about* anxiety. First of all, he makes it clear that only the *experience* of anxiety allows us to enter-tain what is said there. Furthermore, anxiety itself is not what is important in the lecture. It is not taken up to serve as a model, a concrete existence-ideal, but solely with reference to the development of the question of Being.[9] But how is the question of Being approached through the question about meta-physics and what has that to do with the nothing?

In the 1943 postscript to "What is Metaphysics?", Heidegger claims that the question asked in the original lecture arose from a way of thinking that had already entered into the overcoming of metaphysics. But that is far from clear in the original text of the lecture. In the postscript Heidegger says that the ques-tion "What is Metaphysics?" is a question that asks about metaphysics from beyond metaphysics (W 99; EB 380). This might be read as a reference to the first paragraph of the lecture, which renounces *(verzichten)* the question about metaphysics in favor of taking up a specific metaphysical question, that *seems* to leave us within metaphysics (W 1; BW 95). But a resolution of that "seems," so far as the text of the 1929 lecture is concerned, is not sought in a discourse that develops the ambiguity of our stance between the "inside" and "outside" of metaphysics. "Metaphysics," for Heidegger in 1929, no longer simply identi-fies a single discipline within philosophy or even a systematic body of doctrines. It is explicated as "the basic occurrence *(Grundgeschehen)* of *Dasein*" (W 18; BW 112). Metaphysics is presented as something that is always already there so long as man exists; it is not yet understood as an historical epoch, the epoch of Western philosophical thinking, which is the meaning given to it in the post-script.

It is important not to misjudge this important shift in terminology. In an-nouncing the task of "the overcoming of metaphysics" in the 1943 postscript, Heidegger is not calling for the overcoming of what he had still called meta-physics in 1929. This basic occurrence of *Dasein* is what Heidegger had already, in *Being and Time*, called by the name of "clearing" *(Lichtung)* (SZ 133; tr. 171). The clearing in this context means the open of the world as world. In applying the name "metaphysics" to it, Heidegger is playing on its literal sense of "beyond physics" —*meta ta physika* (W 15; BW 109). He is well aware that this was not the historical genesis of the term, which at that time was thought to have arisen from the place Aristotle's collection of treatises on "first philoso-phy" were given in the library organization of his works in the first century before Christ; they followed those entitled "Physics."[10] What Heidegger did was to transform the sense of the "beyond physics." *Dasein* and metaphysics meant the same: passing beyond beings in the sense of being suspended in the nothing. Hence we begin to understand the relation between the experience of anxiety and the question about metaphysics. The insight into the meaning of metaphysics for Heidegger takes place in "the transformation of man into his *Dasein*" (W 10; BW 104). In the 1929 lecture, this is a transformation into what human-being always already is, but from which it for the most part finds itself concealed. This already takes place in anxiety insofar as it is not "you" or "I" who feel ill at ease. It is not only things that slip away in anxiety, but along with them we slip away from ourselves (W 9; BW 102).

Reading "What is Metaphysics?" today, we are in no doubt that when it speaks of the nothing it points to Being. Apparently this was far from clear at the time, except to Japanese readers, who alone recognized *nothing* as a word for Being (US 108–9; WL 19). Heidegger explained it to European readers in his post-script: *Dieses Nichts west als das Sein* (W 101–2; EB 386. VS 144). "Nothing" is a title for Being in the time of the oblivion of Being. If everything one can recognize is only beings, then Being itself, which is not a being, is experienced as nothing. This is what Heidegger means when he says that "Nothingness is the Not of being and thus is Being experienced from the point of view of being" (W 21; EB 3). The Not of being is altogether different from nothingness as *nihil absolutum*. Nor is it a nothing we can arrive at ourselves by negation. We are dealing here with a fundamental experience that arises of its own accord.

How does *nothing* arise as the word for Being? Is it like other words for Being in the history of Being? The postscript to the lecture "What is Metaphysics?" is governed by this recognition of the words of Being and the history of these successive words of Being to which it gives rise. "Obedient to the voice of Being, thinking seeks the word through which the truth of Being comes to language" (W 106; EB 391). The introduction to the lecture, added in 1949 and also known under the title "The Way Back into the Ground of Metaphysics," takes this recognition a step further. The sense in which the overcoming of metaphysics does not oppose metaphysics is clarified. First of all, the overcoming of metaphysics is a matter of destiny and not something we bring about (W 211; WB 221). Second, Being, which was forgotten by metaphysics, can be heard from 'beyond' metaphysics. Only once we are in some sense *outside* metaphysics can we take *the way back into its ground*. This brings about "a change in human nature accompanied by a transformation of metaphysics" (W 197; WB 209). The overcoming of metaphysics is no more and no less than this transformation of metaphysics, the change metaphysics undergoes when it is repeated or gathered in remembrance—so long as we understand that remembrance is only possible once metaphysics has itself come to an end.

But again what is this "end"? And why should remembrance be dependent upon it? How does the insight into metaphysics as the history of the words for Being arise? It would seem that Heidegger's own reflection on his lecture "What is Metaphysics?" was crucial. The experience of the nothing arises in the anxiety in which we are deprived of speech. *Nothing* is not a word for Being alongside the others listed above. The nothing corresponds to the thinker's experience of the lack of a word for Being. This speechlessness, this breaking of the sequence of words for Being, comes to be understood historically as marking the end of the succession of words for Being within metaphysics. What is at issue in the rereading of the lecture is not the description of anxiety, but a particular experience of anxiety that only after the lecture can be identified with any clarity: the anxiety of the thinker who is thwarted in his historical task as a thinker. Through this failure he gains an insight into that historical task, an insight that was denied to previous thinkers. And furthermore this insight takes place as both the culmination and the reversal of previous thinking. It is a culmination in the sense that it fulfills the oblivion of Being. Being withholds itself; it does so throughout metaphysics in the way that none of these words for Being are recognized as such, even by the thinkers who first uttered them. The fulfillment of the withholding of Being is the withholding from the thinker of any word at all. And yet in that very fulfillment, the oblivion of Being is reversed; it is only through the experience in anxiety of the lack of any word for Being at all, that it comes to be recognized that saying Being was the task of the thinker within metaphysics.

The experience of the nothing gives rise to a transformation of thinking that is already exhibited with respect to the very question "what is metaphysics?" itself. I have suggested that the history of Being is metaphysics thought from its end in remembrance. This might give the impression that we can now say what metaphysics is. But this would be to mistake what we are supposed to learn from the history of Being. We might better say that it is an introduction into ambiguity. This is what the transformation of metaphysics amounts to. Metaphysics is both that tradition in all its solidity, though sunk in the oblivion of Being, and at the same time the words through which the truth of Being comes to language. And that is why the confusion that Heidegger recognizes as arising out of his use of the metaphysical word *Being* is unavoidable (US 109; WL 19–20). The manifold meanings of the simple word *Being* at the end of metaphysics include its use by philosophers within the tradition, the sense that it bears in the phrase "words for Being," and 'Being' as experienced in the nothing at the end of metaphysics. To meet these different senses Heidegger introduces a variety of ploys: he writes Being as *Seyn, Seiendheit, Sein*, but the senses cannot always be distinguished. The ambiguity is important to the overcoming of metaphysics itself, because it betrays a necessity that governs thinking. The only words at the thinker's disposal during the time of the overcoming of the tradition are traditional words: we are compelled to speak the old language, as the only language available to us. And it is in submitting himself to the ambiguity of language that the thinker conforms with the transformation of language that takes place when the sequence of words for Being breaks off. The transformation of language does not lie in the introduction of a new vocabulary of perspicuous meaning.

3. Renunciation and the Transformation of *Logos*

In the years following the delivery of the lecture "What is Metaphysics?",
Heidegger came to recognize the extent to which the loss of speech in anxiety
was fundamental to the experience of the nothing. This loss had already been
noticed in the lecture, but it had not provided the central focus. Heidegger had
said, as we saw earlier, that "because beings as a whole slip away, so that just the
nothing crowds round, in the face of anxiety all utterance of the 'is' falls silent."
When we read this sentence today the "because" is immediately questionable.
It seems to say that words disappear because beings slip away. Heidegger would
later recognize that the loss of the thing arises from the lack of the word. But if
we turn to the second part of the sentence, the statement that "the utterance
of the 'is' falls silent" cannot be read today without recalling the lack of the
word for Being.

I have already suggested how Heidegger came to think that it was in the lack
of a word for Being that the insight into the history of philosophy, as a succession of words of Being, arose. Both the postscript and the introduction subsequently added to "What is Metaphysics?" explore the implications of this view
for our conception of metaphysics. The importance of speechlessness for
thinking is recognized in these pages. But, although the postscript acknowledges
that the experience of the nothing is the experience of Being in its oblivion, and
that "the nothing" thus does duty for "Being" in the lecture, the question of the
word *nothing* itself is not raised. What is the status of the "nothing"?
Heidegger's reading of George does not explore the experience of the nothing as
the donation of the word *nothing* as a word for Being; the experience of the
nothing is the experience of the lack of a word for Being. This is the thinker's
experience that Heidegger brings to his reading of George. He learns how the
thinker, like the poet, can still speak and write after the word breaks off. For
though the poet is without the word he sought, he still writes the poem that tells
us of this, and he does it by adopting the language of remembrance and of
renunciation: remembering his previous relation to language and the quest
based upon it, and renouncing it.

In the essay "The Essence of Language," Heidegger offers a double reading
of the final verses of the poem:

> Sadly I learned renunciation:
> Where the word is wanting no thing can be.

According to the first reading, the poet affirms that where the word is lacking
there can be no thing. This means that the word alone gives Being to the thing.
The second reading pays more attention to the fact that the poet says that he is

speaking in the mode of renouncing. What is renounced is again the view that he formerly held of language, whereby the thing stood in a position of priority over the word. But this priority is not now simply reversed. Rather, the poet learns to submit himself to language. He does not so much learn something *about* language, as he learns a different relation to language (US 163-68; WL 60-65). This is taken up again in "The Word" where Heidegger again offers a double reading of the poem. There is a transformation, from the sense in which the poet gives over or denies the claim that he is in a position of mastery over language, to the sense in which the poet gives himself over to the claim *(Anspruch)* of language (US 232-33; WL 151). It is striking that Heidegger is at some pains in both essays, not simply to give first an inadequate reading as a way of clarifying what he takes to be the appropriate reading, but to show how both readings have their place. What I have called here "the first reading" is not only a crucial step on the way to "the second reading"; without it the latter ceases to make any sense.

On first reading, the verse attempts to establish a relation between the presence of the word and the presence of the thing. This is the reading I developed in the first section of this chapter. That reading confines the poem to the language of preserving, a language ruled by presencing *(Anwesen)*. But that neglects the silence of the norn from which the poet learned. If the poet learns from this silence, then silence too belongs to language. Heidegger's name for this language of silence is *das Geläut der Stille* (US 215; WL 108). *Geläut* means "ringing," "peal," or "chime." Heidegger had already introduced this phrase, "the ringing of stillness," in 1950 in the context of a discussion of Trakl. Now he uses it to point to the way that his claims about the relation between word and thing (that language is an origin) and between word and man (that man is not the author and master of language)—claims developed in the course of the dialogue with Hölderlin—must not be understood as the basis for an alternative account of language. They are not supposed to give rise to one more attempt to provide a satisfactory philosophy of language rivaling all previous accounts. They must be drawn back into the experience that gave rise to them and that in turn is the source for a transformation of our relation to language. No doubt Heidegger already knew all that without reading George. But the correspondence between the experience of the poet and the thinker assisted Heidegger in understanding his own experience and the transformation of saying associated with it.

Heidegger's statement in "What is Metaphysics?" that "all utterance of the 'is' falls silent in anxiety" seemed to undergo revision when in "The Essence of Language" he attempted to provide a saying, arising from the thinker's experience of the lack of the word for Being, that corresponds to the final verse of the poem. The saying runs:

Ein "ist" ergibt sich, wo das Wort zerbricht.

An "is" arises where the word breaks up. (US 216; WL 108)

In fact the two sayings complement each other. The "is" that falls silent is the "is" of presencing, 'Being' as it is thought within metaphysics. The "is" that arises is the "is" of the language of Being. In the loss of speech brought on by anxiety in the face of the nothing, something new arises. It arises, according to Heidegger, in a transformation of language, a transformation from the Being of language to the language of Being.

The ambiguity that we have recognized in Heidegger's word *Being* and his reading of George's notion of *renunciation* may be illustrated further in respect of the word *logos*.

The essay "The Word" begins by recalling two lines from Hölderlin's poem *Brot und Wein* (Bread and Wine):

> Warum schweigen auch sie, die alten heilgen Theater?
> Warum freut sich denn nicht der geweihete Tanz?
>
> Why are they also silent, the ancient holy theaters?
> Why does the sacred dance not rejoice?

Heidegger thereby recalls his reading of Hölderlin's poems, which had provided him with his first experience of the dialogue between thinking and poetry. The poem "Bread and Wine" shows that Hölderlin experiences his time as the night in which the gods have fled. According to Hölderlin, the task of the poet has been that of the naming of the gods. Lacking the word to name the gods, he now finds the practice of his vocation disturbed. The saying in which the approach of the god took place is now silenced.

As we saw in the previous chapter, Heidegger read the word *holy* from the poem "*Wie wenn am Feiertage...*" as the word for the realm from which the names for the gods arose. Without repeating this word in his essays on George's poem, Heidegger points to it by following the quotation from Hölderlin's "Bread and Wine" with a passage from Sophocles' *Antigone*. The context of the latter is that Antigone has been confronted by Creon with the fact that she has broken his law, which had been sent to her by his messenger. She replies that it was not Zeus who sent that message. Zeus had sent something else, his law, *ho nomos*. Heidegger translates *ho nomos* as *der weisende Brauch*, the directing use to which humans are put.[11] Heidegger quotes the following lines from Sophocles and offers his own translation:

> ou gar ti nun ge kachthes, all' aei pote
> ze tauta, koudeis oiden ex hotou' phane.

> No one has looked there from
> where it *(ho nomos)* came into radiance.[12]

Zeus's law is one of the ways the god approaches, one of the ways of naming the god in Hölderlin's sense. Hölderlin's word "the holy" names the place from where the law came into radiance; it names the place where, according to Sophocles, no one has looked.

How could Hölderlin do this? What kind of naming is it? The naming of this place is not a naming of something that is present. The name does not even call something absent into presence, for it is the naming of that which itself gives and withholds. Hölderlin can name it only because the gods, whose address normally arises from this place, can no longer be named. The first two sentences of Heidegger's essay "The Word" contrast two places. "From the place we are now let us for a moment commemorate *(andenken)* what Hölderlin asks..." There follows the passage from "Bread and Wine" quoted above. Heidegger then explicates it: "The word is withheld from the former place of the god's appearance, the word as it once was said." Thus before Heidegger even mentions George, he makes the point that this is the time of the gods who have fled. We now enter into a place from which we can look back at a former place, a place where until then no one had looked. Almost effortlessly, with a couple of brief quotations, Heidegger recalls the issues that had occupied him in his reading of Hölderlin, so that his reading of George might be placed within that context. One might say that it is the context of the question of the task of the poet in unpropitious times and, by extension, that of the thinker at the end of the epoch of metaphysics.

The question of the task of thinking at the end of philosophy is pursued in Heidegger's essays on George through the word *logos*. Heidegger, in his interpretation of the poem, insists that we lack the word for the Being of language: "the essence of language nowhere brings itself to word as the language of Being" (US 186; WL 81). But Heidegger only a page earlier referred to *logos* as the name for both Being and saying. Does this not suggest that *logos* is the word for the word?

It is quite possible that Heidegger confronts us with this impasse as to whether *logos* is or is not a word for the Being of language in an effort to provoke us to think about *logos*. In lectures and essays written over a period of some thirty years or more, Heidegger repeated his account of the derivation of the word *logos* from the verb *legein*, which he understands in the sense of "gathering" or "laying." Furthermore, he claimed that what was brought to language with this word was increasingly concealed in the different ways in which it came to be understood, for example, as "speech," "reason," "argument," or "logic." Indeed the oblivion of what is said in the word begins straightaway, according to Heidegger, for although the Greeks dwelt in language as the laying that gathers, they never thought it as such (VA 228; EGT 77). The qualification is perhaps not always made clearly enough, but Heidegger does not, particularly in the last years, offer his interpretation of *logos* as a guide to what the Greeks *meant* by the word. It serves as an indication of how language itself speaks—by a trace at the beginning of philosophy—of the gathering that takes place at the end of philosophy.

To be sure, the dilemma facing the reader of Heidegger's essays on George's poem still remains; however many hundreds of years it has taken, *logos* still emerges as a word for the Being of language. In the course of his reading of George's poem Heidegger had brought to light the close relation between Being and language. What we would say about *logos* as a word for Being, applies to it equally as a word for the word. The history of Being, and thus *logos* as a word for Being, comes to light only at the end of philosophy, the end of the epoch of metaphysics. Its recognition as a word for Being coincides with the end of the rule of *logos; logos* is a word for Being as *das Anwesen des Anwesenden* (US 237; WL 155).

The end of the epoch of metaphysics is the end of the rule of *logos* understood in terms of presencing. At the time of that end, a transformation of language takes place, to which Hölderlin, with his word *hymnos*, is a witness (ED 74). It takes place in George's poem *Das Wort* as "renunciation." In Heidegger's thinking it occurs as the ability to hear what is said by such words for Being as *logos*. Heidegger's phrase for language in the transformed sense is *das Geläut der Stille*—"the ringing of stillness"—because in the silence of the lack of the word for Being, previous words begin to echo from afar.

The transformation of language is more a matter of hearing differently than of speaking differently. For Heidegger, we speak only by listening to language speaking, listening to the prior grant of language. For us, this means learning to hear the withholding of language. As the seeing of what is hidden is called *phenomenological*, so the hearing of the sounds of silence might also be given the same name. The word *logos* withholds itself in a twofold manner. First, within metaphysics it withheld itself as a word for Being by being distorted under the various forms we have mentioned—word, reason, logic, and so on. Second, outside metaphysics *logos* withholds itself insofar as Being no longer holds sway as presencing: "We have to concede that the treasures of language cannot be given artificial currency in a usage somehow refurbished" (WD 99; tr. 153). We come to hear *logos* differently so that it no longer corresponds to "presencing," but speaks according to *das Geläut der Stille*. Although it may no longer be at our disposal to take up in the manner exercised by previous thinkers, the *logos* does not lose its sway; "thinking receives its essential character to this day from what in Greek is called *legein* and *logos*" (WD 102; tr. 163).

The two forms of *logos* correspond to the places of the opening page of the essay: the former place of the god's appearance, the place of Sophocles and of metaphysics, and the place where we are now, the place of Hölderlin and George. Under the thrust of Heidegger's thinking, the two places come together in their proximity; that is to say, the beginning of Western thinking seems to be echoed by another beginning. This is most clearly illustrated by the way in which Heidegger rehearses the fundamental words of the tradition in his startling interpretations. The danger would be if these interpretations were ever to become commonplace. In a sense they already seem to be doing so among some "Heideggerians." If, without struggling with the texts, one were to suppose that those texts said straightforwardly what they do in Heidegger's claim, then *das Geläut der Stille* would itself be silenced.

The word *logos* both is and is not a word for the Being of language. The quest for the Being of language passes at the end of metaphysics into the language of Being. And *logos* as heard by Heidegger passes into the language of Being. The language of another beginning is the language of the first beginning remembered. In 1972 Heidegger wrote a thirteen-line poem with the title *Sprache*.[13] In it he asks when words will again be words. The answer he gives is that it will be when they bear us back to the place of ancient owning *(uralter Eignis)* where the ringing of stillness calls.

Heidegger's word for the difference between what is said and what is "unsaid in what is said" is *rift (Riss)*.[14] Rift is the withdrawal, the withholding, the unspoken that accompanies all language and resounds in *das Geläut der Stille*. The recognition—in remembrance—of the history of Being does not mark the withdrawal of Being's withdrawal. It means rather that the silence is to be heard as silence and that the silence comes to permeate all speaking. The rift would thereby be maintained as a rift between the "inside" and "outside" of metaphysics or, better, between the first and another beginning.

NOTES

1. *Unterwegs zur Sprache*, p. 131; trans. *On the Way to Language*, p. 36. For "gathering" see chapter 1, section 2 above.
2. The third lecture on language from this period is "The Way to Language." It is the main text for my essay "The Transformation of Language at Another Beginning," in *Research in Phenomenology* 13 (1983):5–42, and so has not been given separate consideration here.
3. I would like to thank Dorothea von Mücke for providing me with the translation of George's poem that provides the basis for the version given here. "Mark" is the name applied in medieval Germany to the tract of land held in common by a village community. The norns are the female fates of Scandinavian mythology.
4. Professor Biemel, in his account of the poet's first view of language, already credits the word with the power of retention. So far as I am concerned this obscures the sense in which insight into the relation between language and retention is gained through the experi-

ence of the absence of the word, something Biemel himself acknowledges. Of course, the movement away from that conception of language is something that both our interpretations share, although on my account it takes place in the ambiguity of a double reading. It might also be added that Professor Mehta's translation of the phrase *etwas auf der Hand liegendes* as "something obvious," when it is said of the "treasure," also serves to obscure Heidegger's reading of the poem. W. Biemel, *Martin Heidegger in Selbstzeugnissen und Bilddokumenten* (Hamburg: Rowohlt, 1973), p. 130-31; trans. J. L. Mehta, *Martin Heidegger. An Illustrated Study* (New York: Harcourt Brace Jovanovich, 1976), pp. 154-55.

5. K.-H. Volkmann-Schluck, "Das Problem der Sprache," *Die Frage Martin Heideggers,* hrsg. H.-G. Gadamer, (Heidelberg: Carl Winter, 1969), p. 55; trans. R. Phillip O'Hara, "The Problem of Language", *Martin Heidegger in Europe and America,* ed. G. Ballard and C. E. Scott, (The Hague: Martinus Nijhoff, 1973), p. 124.

6. "Das Seiende spricht nicht mehr an," *Wegmarken,* Gesamtausgabe Band 9 (Frankfurt: Klostermann, 1976), p. 111a. There is a problem in dating the marginalia. The *Gesamtausgabe* gives the edition of the text in which Heidegger's comment is found; obviously this offers only an indication of the date before which it cannot have been written. This particular remark was found in the 1949 edition.

7. Compare Soren Kierkegaard, *The Concept of Anxiety* trans. R. Thomte (Princeton: Princeton University Press, 1980), p. 124: "Inclosing reserve is precisely muteness. Language, the word, is precisely what saves, what saves the individual from the empty abstraction of inclosing reserve."

8. *Wegmarken* (1967), p. 13; trans. *Basic Writings,* p. 108. A similar line of thought is at work in the discussion of anxiety in *Sein und Zeit,* p. 184-85; trans. *Being and Time,* p. 229.

9. *Kant und das Problem der Metaphysik* (Frankfurt: Klostermann, 1951), p. 214; trans. J. Churchill, *Kant and the Problem of Metaphysics* (Bloomington, Ind.: Indiana University Press, 1968), p. 246. Also *Metaphysische Anfangsgründe der Logik in Ausgang von Leibniz,* Gesamtausgabe Band 26 (Frankfurt: Klostermann, 1978), p. 214-15.

10. *Kant und das Problem der Metaphysik,* p. 16; trans, *Kant and the Problem of Metaphysics,* pp. 10-11. This view has now become the subject of dispute. See W. Schulz, "Metaphysik I," in *Die Religion in Geschichte und Gegenwart,* 3. Auflage (Tubingen: J. C. B. Mohr, 1960), Band 4, p. 909.

11. *Brauch* is the word Heidegger uses to translate *to chreon* in Anaximander. He refers to Augustine's *frui. Holzwege,* pp. 338-39; trans. *Early Greek Thinking,* pp. 52-53. Heidegger translates Parmenides *chre* by *es brauchet,* for which the English might be "it is fitting." *Was heisst Denken?,* pp. 113 seq.; trans. *What Is Called Thinking?,* pp. 186 seq. It has the sense of claiming one for a use to which one is fitted.

12. Sophocles *Antigone* 1. 156-57.

13. *Aus der Erfahrung des Denkens,* Gesamtausgabe Band 13, hrsg. H. Heidegger (Frankfurt: Klostermann, 1983), p. 229. German text with a translation by Thomas Sheehan may also be found in *Philosophy Today,* 1976, p. 291.

14. *Unterwegs zur Sprache,* pp. 251 seq.; trans. *On the Way to Language,* pp. 120 seq. Cf. *Der Ursprung des Kunstwerkes,* p. 51; trans. *Poetry, Language, Thought,* p. 63. See also J. Derrida, "Le retrait de la métaphore," *Poésie,* Autumn 1978, pp. 123-26; trans. "The *Retrait* of Metaphor," *Enclitic* 2, no. 2 (1978):30-33.

Chapter Five
The Saying of a Turning:
Heidegger and Technology

1. The Essence of Truth and the Truth of Essence

The first of Heidegger's essays on George's poem *Das Wort* is called *Das Wesen der Sprache*, the essence or nature of language. What is at issue, in the first instance, is the question of what language is as language, the question of the Being of language. The Being of language is a central question for phenomenology in Heidegger's sense of letting what is hidden appear as hidden (SZ 35; tr. 59). What makes the subject a particularly appropriate one for phenomenological investigation is the way language for the most part conceals itself by directing us away from itself toward that which is spoken about. That means that we cannot examine language as language head on. When we speak about language, it is, as something spoken about, reduced to the status of a thing. However correct what we might say about language is, the Being of language belongs more to our speaking than to anything we can say about it. All attempts to put what is spoken about to one side, so that we may concentrate on language, simply dissolve language by reducing it to mere sounds.

If we are to hear language so that it itself says the Being of language, we must come to entertain the withholding of the Being of language (US 186; WL 81). But the event whereby the Being of language, which previously had withheld itself, *appears* as withholding itself, is, for Heidegger an event in the destiny of thinking. It is not simply something we ourselves may bring about; it is the same event as that whereby *aletheia* comes to be heard as *a-letheia*, the entry into the recognition of the history of Being, the language of Being as it is recorded in the words for Being. It might seem that when Heidegger offers the formula *Das Wesen der Sprache: Die Sprache des Wesens*, "the essence of language: the language of essence," he is indicating how, at the time of the end of philosophy, reflection on the essence of language passes into the question about the language of Being or of essence (US 200; WL 94).

That there is more to it than that is apparent from a similar saying to the one on language that is to be found in a note added in 1949 to the essay "On the

Essence of Truth." It runs *Das Wesen der Wahrheit ist die Wahrheit des Wesens*, "the essence of truth is the truth of essence" (W 96; BW 140).[1] Heidegger does not say here that the question of the truth of essence arises out of the question of the essence of truth, but the other way round: "the question of the essence of truth arises from the question of the truth of essence." In other words, Heidegger is expressly cautioning us from attempting to refer the unusual phrase "truth of essence" to the familiar notion of an "essence of truth." In the remainder of this section, I shall, through a reading of the essay "On the Essence of Truth," explore the sense in which the apparently novel question of "the truth of essence" is supposed to have a "priority" over the question of the essence of truth. I shall do this in anticipation that it will serve to clarify the transformation of language described in the parallel saying about the language of essence. Heidegger calls such sayings "sayings of a turning *(Kehre)*." *Kehre* here does not refer to an ostensible shift in Heidegger's own intellectual development, but to an event in the history of Being, the event that brings the insight into the history of Being and thus brings us to the overcoming of metaphysics. The *Kehre* is the turning from metaphysics to another beginning.

The essay "Of the Essence of Truth" begins—as Heidegger so often does—with the "ordinary conception" of what is to be investigated. The ordinary conception of truth is the correspondence theory and Heidegger's first step is to remind us that, of the two versions, the adequation of thing to understanding and the adequation of understanding to thing, it might seem that it is the former that has preeminence. It was so in the transcendental conception of Kant; it was also the case for Aquinas, where it was God's understanding that provided the standard. Both thinkers mean something very different by "the correspondence of thing to understanding," but both believe that it provides the conditions for the possibility of propositional truth. Heidegger only sketches these positions and then even more swiftly dismisses them as theological. Tracing this notion of truth back to its pure philosophical roots in Greek thought, truth is the accordance of statement with thing—propositional truth (W 78; BW 122).

Taking up again the question of the ground of the possibility of truth as the correctness of assertions, Heidegger in the second section of the essay finds that ground in the openness of comportment. Only if we posit an open region within which thing and statement might agree can we account for the supposed agreement of two "things" so different. The essence of truth, he continues in the third section, is "freedom" in the sense of being free for what is opened up in the open region. What first makes correctness possible, and hence is more "original" than it, must be taken as the essence of truth.[2] Heidegger emphasizes the strangeness of this answer in contrast to the supposed obviousness of the traditional tendency to refer propositional truth to the more primordial version of the *adaequatio* with its theological roots. The later notion of *Gelassenheit* or releasement is here clearly anticipated in the discussion of openness; indeed

Heidegger even uses the word to characterize philosophical thinking's refusal to deny the concealment of beings as a whole (W 94; BW 138). Nevertheless it has to be emphasized that the whole account up to this point remains embedded in a transcendental approach. The formulation of the question of truth in terms of its conditions of possibility remains essentially metaphysical and determined by the notion of grounding reason.

Heidegger concedes that his thinking seems to remain on the path of metaphysics, but he asks us to believe that in the passage from truth as correctness to "ek-sistent" freedom, and from freedom to truth as concealing and as errancy, a change in the questioning is accomplished so that it comes to belong to the overcoming of metaphysics (W 97; BW 140-1). We are being prepared for a transformation of thinking (W 83; BW 127). A marginal note added to Heidegger's own copy of the text identifies the space between sections 5 and 6 as the place of the leap into the turning *(Kehre)*, in other words, the passage from "the essence of truth" to "the truth of essence."[3] This is not the occasion to try and follow the intricacies of Heidegger's discussion of errancy. For present purposes it is enough to recognize that at the beginning of section 6 Heidegger introduces the claim that "the concealment of beings as a whole is older than every openness of this or that being" (W 89; BW 132). Heidegger is referring here to the concealment of concealing itself. It is the *lethe* of *a-letheia* as explored in chapter 2 above. Because the always prior concealment of concealment deforms the traditional notion of essence, Heidegger introduces us to 'non-essence' *(Un-wesen)* as essential to the essence. Having introduced it, he then—on the grounds that it might seem contrived—renounces *(verzichtet)* it. This renunciation, like the renunciation he will later embrace in his reading of George, arises because language must not be forced; there must be a listening to language. One does not simply transcend metaphysics by introducing a concept that makes no sense to metaphysics. The language remains metaphysical precisely because an attempt is made to leave metaphysics behind through taking charge of language; this tight grasp maintains a metaphysical attitude to language. And yet the renunciation does not leave everything as it was beforehand. It is not as if the word had never been said. It is not *in spite of* this renunciation, but *through* the "unsaying" that takes place in renunciation that "for those who know about such matters the 'non-' of the primordial non-essence of truth, as untruth, points to the still unexperienced domain of the truth of Being...." (W 90; BW 133).

Already in Section 4, Heidegger had introduced the theme of history: "History begins only when beings themselves are expressly drawn up into their concealment and conserved in it" (W 85; BW 129). So when he says that the concealment of beings is "older" than every openness of this or that being, or when he writes of the "primordial non-essence of truth," we are alerted to the fact that what is at issue is not some temporal priority, but what he would else-

where call a "trace," which is "prior" to history. Heidegger, in this essay, allows
that the essence of truth is determined by history, something inconceivable
within a traditional framework where essences are unchanging and perennial.
The transformations of truth that constitute the history of metaphysics are not
simply the record of a variety of different views about the essence of truth.
They are to be referred to that conception of history that had arisen in the
dialogue with Hölderlin and had led him to say that "history is seldom." "The
rare *(selten)* and the simple decisions of history arise from the way the original
essence of truth essentially unfolds" (W 86; BW 130). But the point is that it
unfolds according to that concealment of concealment that culminates in our
own times when the openness of beings—and thus the essence of truth—is
forgotten (W 88; BW 131). The recognition of the essence of truth as self-
concealing only arises in this culmination and appreciation of the history that
gives rise to it. The passage from the essence of truth to the truth of essence is
therefore not one that completely leaves behind the metaphysical discussion of
truth. Only insofar as it holds to that discussion in remembrance does it sustain
itself, although in the process it comes to see that discussion differently.

In a note appended to the second edition of the essay (1949), Heidegger
provides a brief guide as to how the words in the saying about truth are to be
read. In the phrase "essence of truth," *essence* means initially *quidditas* ("what-
ness") or *realitas*, and *truth* is to be regarded as a characteristic of knowledge.
On the other hand, *essence* in the phrase "truth of essence" is to be understood
verbally, as "essencing." It is not equivalent to *Being* as it is thought throughout
metaphysics, that is, as the Being of beings; it means "the *way* it is thought":
das Wesende des Seins des Seienden. Truth in the phrase "the truth of essence"
means, we are told, "the sheltering that lightens" *(lichtendes Bergen)* as the basic
character of Being. "The essence of truth" is therefore in the first instance to be
read according to its metaphysical sense. Throughout metaphysics Being is
sheltered, in the sense of being concealed. At the end of metaphysics, this concealing, which has determined the essence of truth throughout, is revealed as so
determining the essence of truth. "The essence of truth" comes to be recognized
as meaning the way truth essentially unfolds throughout the history of Being.
This "essential unfolding" can no longer be thought of in terms of something
permanent, "essence" in its traditional sense; it is "essence" in its verbal sense.

There is in the saying "the essence of truth is the truth of essence" a transformation in the essence of truth. But it is not a transformation in the sense that we
see it in Descartes, for example. Those transformations take place *within* metaphysics whereby one conception of truth gives way to another; for example,
truth as the correctness of the proposition gives way to truth as the certainty
of representational thinking (NII 425; EP 23). Rather, it refers to the insight
that those changes are determined by the concept of essence, if it is understood
that "essence" is there serving as a surrogate for what Heidegger calls "Being":

"In the concept of 'essence' philosophy thinks Being" (W 96; BW 139). When Heidegger says that "remembrance in the history of Being thinks history as the arrival, always remote, of the perdurance of truth's essence" (NII 481; EP 75), and that "the possibilities of the actual *concepts* of truth are delineated in advance by the manner of the *essence* of truth and the prevailing of this essence" (NII 490; EP 82-83), it may sound like the Hegelian teleological conception of history. But what is being spoken about is not the arrival of an illumination, but the predominance of a concealment. What arrives is the recognition of the concealment of concealment, but this does not take place as the dissolution of all concealment. It is a question of finding ourselves—in our thinking and our saying—in another, more intimate, relation to it. And this intimacy is most clearly displayed in the new relation that is taken to the previous history of thinking. It is not the case that "the essence of truth" as thought traditionally is now to be dismissed, as if a tradition were something that could be shaken off. What is meant is that the arrival of the truth of essence serves as our entrance into the essence of truth. We now hear the words "essence of truth" so that they no longer speak of an encompassing presence, but are governed by a concealment. And far from that concealment being something new that has only just arrived, it is "older" than the history that begins when beings themselves are drawn up into their unconcealment. That is the framework that allows Heidegger to say that the arrival of the truth of essence serves as our entrance into the essence of truth. We only come to take possession of the language of metaphysics in the sense of hearing what it says, when we renounce ever possessing it in the sense of having mastery over it. And we hear what it says when we recognize that language does not only bring to unconcealment under the sway of a hierarchy ordered by abstract universal essences, but is permeated by an all-pervading power of concealment.

2. Technology and the Break with Essence as Permanent Enduring

In the second edition (1949) of the essay "On the Essence of Truth," Heidegger announced that it was to have been completed by a second lecture "On the Truth of Essence." He indicated that an explanation of the difficulties that stood in the way of this lecture could be found in "The Letter on Humanism." What we find when we turn to "The Letter on Humanism" (1947) is an account of why the third division of the first part of *Being and Time* had never appeared: "The section in question was held back because thinking failed in the adequate saying of this turning and did not succeed with the help of the language of metaphysics" (W 159; BW 208). The turning was in the first instance the reversal of the terms of the title to read "Time and Being," but the reference to the language of metaphysics shows how much more was at issue. "The

Letter on Humanism" then refers explicitly to the essay "On the Essence of Truth" as providing an insight into the turning: "This turning is not a change of standpoint from *Being and Time*, but in it the thinking that was sought first arrives at the location of that dimension out of which *Being and Time* is experienced, that is to say, experienced from the fundamental experience of the oblivion of Being."

I have attempted to indicate how "On the Essence of Truth" might be read so as to provide an insight into this experience. And yet without the companion essay "On the Truth of Essence," the account of the turning clearly remains incomplete and, one must presume, for the same reasons that *Being and Time* remained incomplete. We find further clarification of these reasons later in the essay when Heidegger writes of the attempt to think the truth of Being and the difficulty he encounters of finding a language that retains "the essential help of phenomenological language" (W 187; BW 235). He acknowledges that all attempts to say more than philosophy could say are confronted by the limitation that "in order to make the attempt at thinking recognizable and at the same time understandable for existing philosophy, it could at first be expressed only within the horizon of that existing philosophy and its use of current terms." That much is clear, but it is not simply a question of finding a language that is intelligible to one's audience. It might seem that the reason why all inquiries into Being must at first introduce themselves as metaphysical—as we have seen both with "What is Metaphysics?" and "On the Essence of Truth"—is the more pressing one that in the West the only language available to the thinker is that of metaphysics. And yet we have also seen how, for example in the treatment of *logos* in the essays on George, it is discovered that the task is not to conjure up a new language from somewhere in order to express these new revelations. Language itself, so long as we listen to it, has already responded to the truth of Being.

An even clearer illustration of this is provided by an important lecture dating from the early 1950s, "The Question concerning Technology." It provides us with an opportunity to observe the transformation that the word *Wesen* undergoes in the context of modern technology. "It is technology itself that makes the demand on us to think in another way what is usually understood by 'essence'" (VA 38; BW 311). Heidegger's approach to technology is in the first instance to restore it to its historical context. A number of commentators have insisted that one of Heidegger's great achievements has been to show the extent to which the beginning of modern technology can already be found in Greek metaphysics.[4] Certainly Heidegger claims this as part of his account of the unity of metaphysics, but it is important to recognize that the fundamental thesis of the essay on technology is, by contrast, that notwithstanding the long preparation for technology within the history of metaphysics, the traditional concepts no longer appear to hold, no longer seem to be applicable for modern machine-powered technology (VA 21; BW 295).

The specific example that Heidegger provides of the breakdown of traditional concepts in the face of technology is *poiesis*. He interprets it as "bringing-forth." Not only the making of a craftsman, an artist, or a poet, but also the rising up of "nature" *(physis)* is described as *poiesis*. The Greek understanding of *physis*, both in Plato and Aristotle, is illuminated by an understanding of *poiesis*.[5] This foreshadows the time of technology, when nature is reduced to supplying the materials for making and providing a source of energy to sustain that making process. Indeed *poiesis* is more than an example for Heidegger; the fundamental characteristic of presencing in metaphysics is *poiesis* in its various forms (SD 49; TB 46). It is revealing as a bringing-forth from concealment to unconcealment. Since the time of his reading of Aristotle's *Nicomachean Ethics* in the early 1920s, Heidegger had recognized *aletheia* as the name for such revealing. The clue that lay behind Heidegger's discovery that *aletheia* meant more than its conventional translation of "truth" suggests, was the fact that Aristotle had written of the *aletheia* not only of theoretical knowledge, but also of *praxis* and *poiesis*.[6] The Greek word for the kind of knowing involved in *poiesis* is *techne*—hence "technology." If "phenomenological seeing" can show us that modern technology witnesses the breakdown of this conceptual schema, the repercussions will be enormous.

First, we must look at the account that Heidegger gives of technology. Heidegger points to the transformation of agriculture into the mechanized food industry and to the "unlocking" of nature when it is made into an energy source that can be stored, in order to introduce the notion of challenging *(Herausfordern)*. But it is not only that man challenges nature, he himself is challenged: "Only to the extent that man for his part is already challenged *(herausgefordert)* to exploit *(herauszufordern)* the energies of nature can this disclosing which orders happen" (VA 25; BW 299). For Heidegger, this challenge, although very different from *poiesis*, is also a disclosing *(Entbergen)*. Heidegger gives to the disclosing of challenging the name *Ge-stell*. It is usually translated as "enframing," but because this conveys very little to the English reader I shall retain the German word.[7] The challenge of *Ge-stell* claims man for technology. One might object that one is not aware of any such claim *(Anspruch)* and Heidegger concedes this. Indeed it is absolutely central to his account. "Man stands so decisively in attendance on the challenging-forth of *Ge-stell* that he does not grasp *Ge-stell* as a claim, that he fails to see himself as the one addressed" (VA 35; BW 308). Disclosing, whether it be that of *poiesis* or that of challenging, has always already transferred us into the unconcealed, so that the claim only acts anonymously and we fail to be aware of it as such (VA 27; BW 300).

Heidegger's attempt to enable us to recognize that even in technology humanity is claimed by Being begins by acknowledging that this is not our immediate experience: "it seems as though man everywhere and always encounters only himself" (VA 35; BW 308). His posture of being "lord of the earth" encourages him in the illusion that everything he encounters is his own

construct. Here Heidegger is referring to much more than the familiar observa-
tion that the inhabitants of large cities live in a man-made environment. We are
concerned with the counterpart of the philosophical thesis that "man is the
measure of all things."[8] We find it reflected, for example, in the means-ends
structure insofar as it is directed to an ordering provided by man. But, for
Heidegger, that man encounters only himself is "the final delusion." It is the
culmination of the history of the growing oblivion of Being, and Heidegger would
say that in technology human beings preeminently fail to encounter themselves
in their essence—granted that their essence is to be claimed by Being (W 155;
BW 204). And yet here in technology, human beings are addressed by Being, as
much as they are anywhere. It is a matter of recognizing technology as itself an
epoch in the destiny of Being.

The essay on technology pursues the consequences of this account of the
claim, more than it sets out to persuade its readers to see the claim. This latter
task is pursued elsewhere, for example in a speech delivered at his birthplace
Messkirch on the occasion of its seventh centenary.

> Everyone is familiar with the phenomena of technological production.
> We look at them with astonishment. And yet no one knows what in truth
> this thing is by which man today is being challenged in increasing degree
> to such boundless activity. What overpowers man in this way can itself be
> no mere human product. For this reason it remains puzzling and
> uncanny.[9]

Modern technology is such that we can no longer suppose that human beings are
in control of it or that they have its measure. They experience this in the boredom that afflicts them, boredom not just in relation to this or that, but in the
fact that nothing appeals any longer; "things" have lost their power to address
us. Heidegger envisages a time when the boredom and indifference become so
all-consuming, our attempts to divert ourselves from it so far-reaching that no
one would even recognize any longer what "homeland" meant and so, equally,
the alien would no longer be recognized as such. The parallel between this
cultural, or rather "epochal," experience and the more individual one of anxiety,
as it is described in "What is Metaphysics?", is clear.

And Heidegger's treatment of this boredom in the face of the technological
world is similarly an attempt to look behind the surface phenomena of technology. The procedure he uses is no more than a variation on a practice that he
had exercised throughout his thinking. In *Being and Time*, Heidegger had
insisted that "falling"—a preoccupation with everyday concerns and an absorp-
tion in what "everyone" is saying—discloses *Dasein* as that in the face of which
Dasein itself flees (SZ 184-85; tr. 229). In "What is Metaphysics?" compulsive

chatter is understood in relation to the silence that it serves to conceal; chatter comes to provide evidence of the nothing (W 9-10; BW 103). These are examples of "phenomenological seeing" in Heidegger's sense of letting what lies hidden appear as hidden (Cf. SZ 35; tr. 59) and, although one can only make the identification tentatively, it is the kind of "phenomenological" seeing that Heidegger had said—in the passage from "The Letter on Humanism" quoted above—was essential for advancing the thought of the truth of Being. In the talk given at Messkirch, boredom and the consequent search for something to pre-occupy one is recognized by Heidegger as a hidden homesickness. "Thus in all (the forms of) the alien there yet comes towards us the homeland that we seek, even though it is wrapped in disguise."[10] We have not yet reached the stage when we no longer know what the homeland was.

When we return to "The Question concerning Technology," we find a similar attempt at a "phenomenological" description, although admittedly at a higher level of complexity than that found in the Messkirch speech. The basis for the illusion that man encounters only himself is the obstruction or blocking *(Verstellen)* of *poiesis* (VA 38; BW 311). But Heidegger raises the question as to whether we cannot find there a source of testimony about the nature of revealing that provides an unsuspected insight into it. Heidegger's attempt to do this takes place in an account of the transformation in the notion of *Wesen* that accompanies technology. One sentence in particular provides the best guide to how technology makes the demand on us to think in another way what is usually understood by "essence."

> Wie die Technik west, lässt sich nur aus jenem Fortwähren ersehen, worin sich das Ge-stell als ein Geschick des Entbergens ereignet.

> The way in which technology essences, lets itself be seen only on the basis of the permanent enduring, in which *Ge-stell* comes to pass as a destining of revealing. (VA 39; BW 312)

If we adopt the word *essentia* for the concept of essence that is being challenged and we retain the word *Wesen* for the understanding of essence that arises from the challenge, we can remove, as a temporary expedient, the "ambiguity" of *Wesen* at the time of technology. The justification for doing so lies simply in the hope that by so doing we may come to a deeper appreciation of the ambiguity that embraces language at the time of the turning. *Essentia* and *Wesen* are both ways of enduring. *Essentia* alone, according to Heidegger, is meant as a permanent enduring. With the advent of technology, *essentia* passes to *Wesen*. *Ge-stell*, which is Heidegger's name for the essence of technology, essences as *Wesen*. Consequently the above sentence may be rewritten to read as follows:

> *Wesen* lets itself be seen from *essentia* wherein *Ge-stell* comes to pass as a destining of revealing.

The sentence tells how the demand on the thinker to think *Wesen* in place of *essentia* rises not through something external, but through *essentia* itself. This does not mean that *Wesen* can be thought in terms of *essentia*. Were that the case, there would be no demand to think essence differently. But the thinking of *essentia* is the site of the advent of *Ge-stell*, which cannot be thought in terms of *essentia*.

The last phrase of the sentence, which says that "*Ge-stell* comes to pass as a destining of revealing," recalls the history of Being. In metaphysical thought, revealing is governed by *poiesis*. But with the advent of *Ge-stell*, *poiesis* is blocked off *(verstellt)*. That is to say, its revealing is concealed, in the same sense that Being is forgotten in the modern era. But, of course, the whole of metaphysics is, according to Heidegger, characterized by the oblivion of Being. "All coming to presence *(alles Wesende)*, not only modern technology, keeps itself everywhere concealed to the last" (VA 30; BW 303). Throughout the tradition, revealing is as such concealed in favor of the concentration on beings. So if Heidegger is to insist that "ordering" *(bestellen)*, which is what he calls the revealing that takes place in technology, is concealed, we must try to elucidate the sense in which it is preeminently concealed and not just concealed in the same manner as all metaphysical revealing.

Heidegger attempts to elucidate this difference with the phrase *die Verweigerung von Welt*, "the refusal of world" (TK 46; QT 49). The obstruction of *poiesis*, exhibited for example in the circularity of consumption for the sake of consumption, is characterized elsewhere by Heidegger in the phrase "the history of the world which had become an unworld" (VA 96; EP 107). But because the history of Being has taken place in the "worlding of the world," this refusal of world also amounts to refusal of the truth of Being (TK 45; QT 48). But it is precisely in the silence of refusal that Heidegger awaits recognition of the truth of Being, recognition of the indestructible belongingness of man within granting. We can reasonably conjecture that this insight arises by the same kind of "phenomenological seeing" at work in "What is Metaphysics?" and the speech delivered at Messkirch. What is striking though is that in the essay "The Question concerning Technology," the analysis is directed not to a mood, but to language. It is in an experience to be undergone with language that Heidegger on this occasion seeks to introduce us to the turning *(Kehre)*.

The watchword of Heidegger's attempt is provided by lines drawn from Hölderlin's poem *Patmos:*

> Wo aber Gefahr ist, wächst
> Das Rettende auch.

But where the danger is, grows
The saving-power also.

There is no skirting the extreme difficulty of what Heidegger is inviting us to experience. I must also emphasize the extreme tentativeness with which he always introduces it. As a commentator, one tends to pass over it. But unless the danger is recognized as such, then there is no passage to the saving power. If there were no uncertainty, there would be no danger. Yet the danger is all-consuming: it is Being itself, the epoch of Being, unfolding as *Gestell* (TK 42; QT 43).

The culmination of Heidegger's essay on technology is the treatment of "essence." *Poiesis* in metaphysics comes to conform to *essentia* as a genus or a *quidditas*. Even the Greek understanding, which is different, has it that all revealing takes place according to that which abides, the *eidos* of the *aei on. Essence* means "permanent enduring." But this account of essence cannot be sustained within the context of the experience of technology. And this is most apparent in the experience we undergo with the word itself. "If we speak of the 'essence of a house' and the 'essence of a state' we do not mean a generic type; rather we mean the ways in which house and state hold sway, administer themselves, develop, and decay – the way in which they 'unfold' *wesen*" (VA 38; BW 312). The change in the account of "essence" given by various philosophical schools is well documented, but perhaps philosophers still reflect too little on the meaning of such a change, too eager perhaps to account for it by reference to superior application of a method, for example. Heidegger invites us to recognize this change as a historical destiny.

The "new" concept of essence is not one that Heidegger would have us adopt as a matter of preference. It is not unambiguously "new"; the way in which technology essentially unfolds can only be seen because we hold to *essentia* in remembrance. The device of trying to separate two different senses of "essence" must now be relinquished so that we can restore to the name *Ge-stell*, as the title of the essence of technology, its proper ambiguity – an ambiguity that does not have its source in the "coincidence" of two distinct meanings in a single term. *Ge-stell* is precisely the double aspect of the danger and the saving power. It has, Heidegger says, a Janus-head (SD 57; TB 53) so that the word *Ge-stell* is itself the saying of a turning; it is at the farthest extreme of metaphysics, the final delusion, and yet it moves to another understanding by remembering the previous understanding. "The essence of technology is in a lofty sense ambiguous. This ambiguity points to the mystery of all revealing, i.e., of truth" (VA 41; BW 314).

3. The Saying of a Turning and the Speculative Proposition

With the saying of a turning, Heidegger sought a way of speaking other than that of ordinary assertions, just as Hegel had with his speculative proposition already challenged the dominance of the assertion in philosophical writing. The question of Heidegger's proximity to Hegel now arises in respect of their language.

Hegel's disucussion of how speculative propositions are to be read occurs in the Preface to the *Phenomenology of Spirit*. Both the form and the content of a speculative proposition are such that the reader cannot find a firm footing at any point. He goes back and forth between subject and predicate confounded, and thereby stays with the subject matter. "Thinking therefore loses the firm objective basis it had in the subject when, in the predicate, it does not return into itself, but into the subject of the content."[11] The reader experiences a disordering of directionality. This inhibition or restraint *(Hemmung)*, this counterthrust *(Gegenstoss)* and being thrown back *(zuruckwerfen)* constitute the experience of reading a speculative proposition.

The speculative proposition is given the task of elucidating what is essential. Although it looks like an ordinary proposition, so that we approach it as we would any subject-predicate proposition, the usual passage we make when we read a sentence is disturbed by its philosophical content. Reading it, we undergo an experience with language. We fail to anticipate that the predicate provides not an attribute of the subject, but its essence. The subject is in the predicate, instead of the predicate belonging to the subject. The firm base that one customarily takes in the subject of the proposition and from which one moves away is lost. When Hegel says "the subject is lost" *(das Subject geht verloren)* he means both that the grammatical subject moves across to the predicate and that the thinking subject is at a loss.[12] Because thinking is disturbed, it does not pass on or become engaged in arguing *(räsonniren)*; it stays with the content. When Hegel criticizes those who complain that philosophy books must be read again and again, he is making the point that if we are held by the proposition, so that we read it again and again, we stay with what is being spoken about. Instead of saying that the subject is lost, Hegel might have said that the subject finds itself. The grammatical subject is found in the predicate as its essence. The thinking subject finds itself held by what is being said.

Certain points of contact between Hegel's speculative proposition and Heidegger's saying of a turning stand out, such as the loss of the standpoint of subjectivity. In both Hegel and Heidegger, this loss takes place in the first instance in being held by the subject matter. At a deeper level we can observe that the speculative proposition arises within a thinking in terms of concepts *(das begreifende Denken)*, for which the opposition between thought and object has been left behind. Heidegger's *Dasein* has equally left the subject-object

distinction behind. Nevertheless there can be no question but that the transformation into *Da-sein* is entirely different from the attainment of absolute
knowing in Hegel. Is that difference reflected in the manner in which the respective propositions should be read?

The reversal that is the predominant aspect of the saying of a turning is also
present in the speculative proposition. Heidegger says of the proposition "the
essence of truth is the truth of essence" that, if one makes allowances for the use
of an "unfortunate grammatical category," the subject of the proposition is
"the truth of essence" (W 96; BW 140). Similarly the transition between
genitivus obiectivus and *genitivus subiectivus* is a feature not just of Heidegger's
saying of a turning. Heidegger has correctly recognized its presence in the
original title of the *Phenomenology of Spirit* – "Science of the Experience of
Consciousness" (H 182; HE 140). Finally, we also find propositions reversed in
Hegel. In the final chapter of the *Phenomenology*, we find alongside the proposition "the being of the 'I' is a thing" the proposition "the thing is 'I.'"[13] The two
propositions, which are called infinite judgments, are drawn from earlier in the
text. Together they mark a transition from the chapter on "Observing Reason"
to the section entitled "The World of Self-Alienated Spirit." Indeed the account
of the speculative proposition in the preface, whereby the grammatical subject
is found in the predicate, may derive from this juxtaposition in the final chapter,
which was written before it.

The saying of a turning speaks as a ringing of stillness *(Geläut der Stille)*.
The phrase "saying of a turning" arises first in a denial, specifically the denial:
"Thinking failed in the inadequate saying of this turning" (W 159; BW 208).
Heidegger succeeds with the saying only when he has learned what George calls
"renunciation." Hence he says that man must learn to exist in the nameless
(W 150; BW 199). In a lecture dating from 1957, Heidegger introduces the
phrase "a saying not-saying" *(sagendes Nichtsagen)* (ID 66; tr. 73). It arises
during a discussion as to whether Western languages can speak nonmetaphy-
sically; Hegel's speculative proposition is mentioned shortly after, but not as an
illustration of a saying not-saying. This is quite correct. On the other hand,
language is the voice of reason in Hegel in a way somewhat parallel to the sense
in which language is the voice of Being in Heidegger. This is exhibited by the
propositions drawn from the tradition that Hegel transforms at the completion
of philosophy by reading them as speculative propositions. The clearest
examples are proposition about God or the soul. In Scholasticism, they are
regarded as a firm basis to which predicates can be attached.[14] A speculative
reading passes beyond that. It reveals in dogmatic assertions the speculative
concept *(Begriff)*, as Heidegger's reading of *logos* or *poiesis* hears in those words
the silent call of Being. Thus "God is absolute" says "the essence of God is the
absolute": "only by virtue of the absoluteness of the Absolute is God essentially
God" (WD 101; tr. 156). How does Hegel understand "essence" here? For

Heidegger, the Hegelian essence of the speculative proposition is firmly placed within the metaphysical tradition. It is "the speculative-absolute essence."[15]

Heidegger regards the dialectical transformation of a proposition like "God is the Absolute" as a transformation within Western thinking. This is because he understands it as a reversal arising from the ambiguity of the form of the proposition such that it can be read either as "*God* is the Absolute" or "*God* is the *Absolute.*" The justification for this reading is that the movement of the speculative proposition takes place when what appears at first as a predicate emerges, in Hegel's words, as "the substance and the essence and Concept of that which is discussed."[16] The Hegelian sense of essence provides the firm basis for the speculative proposition. The saying of a turning takes place in the transition away from the concept of essence that reaches its extreme in Hegel.

The transformed understanding of essence in Heidegger is, in contradistinction to Hegel and the tradition, the loss of a firm standard. The turning is not a turn from one site to another. We do not leave behind the essence of truth, the essence of language or the granting of metaphysics. Just as the question of the Being of language can only be approached through the entrance into the language of Being, just as the question of the essence of truth arises only through the question of the truth of essence, so the question of technology, which brings an insight into the granting of the tradition, arises from the inapplicability of the traditional concept of making to machine-powered technology (VA 21; BW 295).

It might seem curious, this constant repetition of the word *question*. It is no affectation. The reluctance to state the question explicitly is due to the renunciation of the question-form "what is x?", which appears to be asking for an *essentia*, a basis. Thinking is not a putting of questions but an entrance into the prior grant (US 175–76; WL 71–72). If there is a transformation in Heidegger's saying of a turning it is not the adoption of a new basis for thinking, but a transformation of language so that the silent is heard and retained in the saying not-saying.

NOTES

1. The transition from the essence of truth to the truth of essence already takes place in the main body of "On the Essence of Truth," which was based on a lecture delivered in 1930 and before its first publication in 1943 was frequently revised – particularly in respect of what was said there about the truth of essence. The saying that the essence of truth is the truth of essence is already uttered in a subclause in an earlier essay, "Remembrance into Metaphysics," dated 1941 but not published until 1961 (*Nietzsche* II:481; *The End of Philosophy*, p. 75). In addition, Heidegger says in the 1936 lecture on "The Origin of the Work of Art" that he is not there seeking the truth of essence, but the essence of truth (*Der Ursprung des Kunstwerkes*, p. 53; *Poetry, Language, Thought*, p. 50). Nevertheless the note appended to "On the Essence of Truth" in 1949 provides the most important guidance as to how the saying should be read.

2. *Wegmarken*, Gesamtausgabe Band 9, hrsg. F-W. von Herrmann (Frankfurt: Klostermann, 1976), p. 186. The sentence "Das Wesen der Wahrheit ist die Freiheit" (*Wegmarken* [1967], p. 81; *Basic Writings*, p. 125) has become, in spite of the claim that the text is unchanged, *Das Wesen der Wahrheit, als Richtigkeit der Aussage verstanden, ist die Freiheit*. Loscerbo's suggestion that *Richtigkeit* in the third section "does not refer to the correctness of assertion, but rather to the self-directing of Dasein toward beings" cannot therefore be sustained (*Being and Technology* [The Hague: Nijhoff, 1981], p. 187). Loscerbo nevertheless recognizes the provisional character of this statement about the essence of truth even though he is insufficiently attuned to the text's strategy whereby the confrontation with the metaphysical accounts of truth is pursued in the first instance in a manner self-consciously reminiscent of metaphysics (W 97; BW 140). This constraint is imposed by the dual impossibility of either maintaining oneself in the overcoming of metaphysics simply by attempting to take a step outside metaphysics or, alternatively, remaining within it.

3. "Zwischen 5. und 6. der Sprung in die (im Ereignis wesende) Kehre," *Wegmarken*, Gesamtausgabe Band 9, p. 193 n.

4. See, for example, H-G. Gadamer, "Wieweit schreibt Sprache das Denken vor?", *Kleine Schriften* IV (Tübingen: J. C. B. Mohr, 1977), 89; trans. W. Glen-Doepel, *Truth and Method* (London: Sheed & Ward, 1975), p. 494.

5. Certain of Heidegger's scattered remarks about the relation between *poiesis* and *physis* in Aristotle cannot be easily reconciled. The key seems to be that, on Heidegger's reading, Aristotle interprets *physis* in the light of *poiesis*. See especially the protocol to the Zähringen Seminar (1978), *Vier Seminare*, p. 130.

6. Aristotle's *Nicomachean Ethics*, book VI, ch. 2-7, Loeb Classical Library; trans. H. Rackham (London: Heinemann, 1934), pp. 326-43.

7. For a valuable discussion of the attempts to translate *Ge-stell* into French, see M. Haar, "Heidegger et l'essence de la technique," *Revue de l'Enseignement Philosophique* 30, no. 2 (Décembre 1979–Janvier 1980):33 n. 17.

8. See Heidegger's discussion of Protagoras' saying at *Nietzsche* 2:135–41; trans. F. Capuzzi, *Nietzsche: Nihilism* (New York, Harper & Row, 1982), pp. 91–95. Also *Holzwege*, pp. 94–96; trans. W. Lovitt, *The Question concerning Technology* (New York: Harper & Row, 1977), p. 143-45.

9. "Messkirch's Seventh Centennial," trans. T. Sheehan with German text, *Listening* 8 (1973) pp. 46–47. The German text originally appeared under the title "Ansprache zum Heimatsabend am 22. Juni 1961," *700 Jahre Stadt Messkirch* Messkirch, 1962, pp. 7-16.

10. "Messkirch's Seventh Centennial," pp. 52-53.

11. *Phänomenologie des Geistes*, p. 44; trans. A. V. Miller, *Phenomenology of Spirit*, p. 39.

12. In recognizing a double meaning here, I find myself in agreeement with J. P. Surber, "Hegel's Speculative Sentence," *Hegel-Studien*, Band 10, 1975, p. 221.

13. *Phänomenologie des Geistes*, p. 422; trans. *Phenomenology of Spirit*, pp. 480-81.

14. *Enzyklopädie der philosophischen Wissenschaften (1830)*, hrsg. F. Nicolin und O. Pöggeler (Hamburg: Felix Meiner, 1969), sec. 31, pp. 61–62; trans. W. Wallace, *The Logic of Hegel* (London: Oxford University Press, 1968), p. 65.

15. *Hegels Phänomenologie des Geistes*, Gesamtausgabe Band 32, hrsg. I. Gorland (Frankfurt: Klostermann, 1980), p. 193.

16. *Phänomenologie des Geistes*, p. 43; trans. *Phenomenology of Spirit*, p. 37.

Chapter Six
Ereignis: Experience and Remembrance

1. Experience: *Erlebnis* and *Erfahrung*

In the preceding chapters the word *experience* has frequently been used. It receives a certain authorization from Heidegger's own texts. Already in *Being and Time*, Heidegger announced the task of uncovering the primordial experiences of the history of ontology. He came to understand *Being and Time* itself as arising from a single experience, that of the oblivion of Being. His dialogue with George's poem *Das Wort* was directed toward undergoing an experience with language. The examples could be multiplied. Nevertheless the question has sometimes been posed as to whether Heidegger's notion of "experience" does not echo Hegel's. If this was conceded, its significance would not be a matter of settling a specific issue in the history of ideas. If Hegel's notion of "experience" is also Heidegger's, then there would be a prima facie case that the latter remains tied to metaphysical notions at the heart of his attempt to overcome metaphysics. What is Heidegger's understanding of "experience"?

It means something very different from the *experimenta* of a philosophy of experience. *Experimenta* are repeatable, take place under conditions that are set by us, and are public in the sense of being in principle open to the inspection of everyone. They give rise to a form of proof that corresponds to that of argument in the realm of logic. By contrast, experience as Heidegger thinks it is a destiny *(Geschick)*: it is sudden and unique (US 224 and 229; WL 143 and 148). The concept of experience as *Erfahrung* is always carefully distinguished by Heidegger from experience as *Erlebnis*. The latter is usually translated "lived experience" and it is true that the notion of life is an important part of this concept. The word *Erlebnis* originally referred to the way in which experience accumulates a residue over the course of a lifetime.[1] The concept was transformed by Simmel who likened it to an adventure. An adventure begins when an accident breaks up the continuity of one's life; it ends when one returns to the customary context with the proper order restored. Experience in this sense is essentially the reintegration, the healing of the break that previously took place.

The connection with the earlier concept of *Erlebnis* is that in the course of an adventure in this sense, life itself is felt because the everyday has been temporarily left behind.[2] We know that Heidegger read Simmel with enthusiasm during the 1920s and certainly it is Simmel's, not Husserl's, concept of *Erlebnis* that comes closest to Heidegger's *Erfahrung*.

Heidegger brings out the connotation of journeying *(fahren)* that belongs to the word *Erfahrung*. Passing along the way, one attains something: *eundo assequi* (US 169; WL 66). As with the model of adventure, there is a transformation of one's environment. The crucial difference is that whereas with *Erlebnis* understood in terms of the model of adventure, the old order is restored; with *Erfahrung*, after the experience one can never be at ease in the old dispensation.[3] One is oneself transformed (US 159; WL 57). The clear forerunner of this understanding of experience is undoubtedly Hegel, but the distance that Heidegger lets appear between his own usage and that of Hegel is fundamental to understanding how these two thinkers come to experience the history of thinking differently.

Heidegger's essay "Hegel's Concept of Experience" provides the best guide to understanding this difference.[4] Heidegger's essay takes the form of a detailed commentary on the Introduction to the *Phenomenology of Spirit*. The crucial sentence for the interpretation runs: "This *dialectical* movement, which consciousness exercises on itself—on its knowledge as well as on its object—is, *insofar as the new, true object emerges to consciousness* out of it, precisely that which is called *experience*" (PS 60; tr. 55). Nothing seems more natural than an account of experience along these lines. Following such an experience, things are no longer the same for us; we have, it seems, been directed elsewhere. We find subsequently that the transformation that we have suffered in undergoing the experience is a correction of our previous knowledge, which was found to have been inadequate. So an experience that we had regarded as the advent of something quite new is discovered to be an experience of a specific inadequacy out of which the reintegration of consciousness and its new object arises as a determinate negation. A case can be made for saying that this account satisfies what we ordinarily mean when we say that we have undergone an experience. But Hegel—and Heidegger's account brings this out very well—is not concerned with providing an account of what we ordinarily understand by "experience" (H 172; HE 125).

To appreciate Hegel's concept of experience we must place it firmly within the context of the *Phenomenology of Spirit* as the ladder to the standpoint of absolute knowing. "The experience of consciousness," in Hegel's terminology, is not known to natural consciousness. Natural consciousness does not recognize the emergence of the new object from out of the knowing of the first object. Experience is essentially always only "for us," the observers. The identity of the "we" has been the subject of some controversy.[5] For Heidegger the standpoint of the "we," the observers who simply observe the correlation of knowing and object as it takes place within natural consciousness, is attained only in absolute knowing. From the standpoint of absolute knowing, the progressive unfolding of natural consciousness is the "re-membrance" *(Er-Innerung)* of the absolute. As Heidegger puts it, "Experience is the movement of the dialogue between natural and absolute knowing" (H 188; HE 148).

This is not the place to pursue the details of Hegel's text or Heidegger's own dialogue with it. To do so would involve us in a lengthy inquiry into the history of the concept of truth. We would need to show the equilibrium of the *adaequatio* theory of truth in medieval philosophy, its collapse in modern philosophy, and its partial recovery, radically transformed, in Hegel. Heidegger's dense commentary pursues this theme somewhat cryptically. The fundamental claim that Heidegger makes here is that Hegel's word *Erfahrung* is a word for Being (H 165-66; HE 113). As such it belongs alongside such words as *physis, logos, idea, substantiality, objectivity, subjectivity,* and *will*; it belongs in particularly close relation to *subjectivity*. Heidegger is also at pains to emphasize the tie between Hegel's concept of experience and presencing *(Anwesen)*: "Experience, the presentation of the absolute representation, is the *parousia* of the Absolute" (H 171; HE 120-21). *Parousia* means presencing (H 122; HE 34). The word *Phenomenology* that Hegel selects for the title of the work is read by Heidegger to say "the self-gathering of the dialogue between Spirit and its parousia" (H 185; HE 145).

As Heidegger points out, the *Phenomenology of Spirit* was until a late stage to have been called "Science of the Experience of Consciousness."[6] Heidegger speculates as to why Hegel dropped the word *experience* from the title and notices also that the word seems to recede in importance toward the end of the book.[7] He wonders whether Hegel found it too daring to draw this word from the grant of language. As Heidegger says elsewhere: "The difficulty lies not so much in finding the word for Being as in retaining purely in genuine thinking the word found" (H 337-38; EGT 52). Hegel's withdrawal of the word *experience* serves to indicate its place within the history of the oblivion of Being in the same way that the ambiguity of the concept of actuality at the beginning of the modern epoch was presented as the sign of "a genuine transition."[8]

"Experience" in Heidegger does not have the sense of a progressive development as it has in Hegel. For Heidegger, experience almost always takes place in the face of a lack. Heidegger has remarked on the difficulty that metaphysical thinking has had in thinking absence and the nothing. There is a pronounced tendency within the history of metaphysics to posit an entity in the face of a default. Thus hallucination is explained away by positing sense-data and the failure to understand a foreign language gives rise to the positing of meaning-intentions by analytical thinking. The positing of such entities contributes to the concealment of the question of Being. For the phenomenological thinking of

Heidegger, a lack or default gives access to Being. In the preceding chapters, I have sought to examine some of the foremost examples of this from Heidegger's texts: the experience of the nothing in anxiety, which he recognizes as the experience of Being from the point of view of beings; the failure of the poet George, as described in his poem *Das Wort*, to find the word for the word; the experience of the default of the gods, which lets Hölderlin name the holy; how the failure of the traditional concept of essence to describe the experience of modern technology provides the insight into the dominance of presencing and at the same time takes us beyond it. Ultimately these experiences are the same; they are all the experience of the epoch of the withdrawal of Being.

The earliest example in Heidegger's published work of the experience of a lack showing Being is that of the default of an implement that is unusable, missing, or in the way; it gives access to the worldhood of the world (SZ 72-74; tr. 102-4). Heidegger subsequently concedes that the obtrusiveness *(Aufdringlichkeit)* of an implement that has let us down still conceals the Being of the implement itself. Its Being is reliability *(Verlässlichkeit)* and, using Van Gogh's painting of a pair of shoes as his example, it awaits an experience with the work of art to bring it to unconcealment (UK 30-33; PLT 34-36). This does not mean that Being is open to scrutiny in the work of art. The work of art is a site of Being precisely because it is not a simple manifestation; the work of art always has belonging to it an impenetrable depth—a mystery. Art has an important place in Heidegger's thinking because it shows concealment and unconcealment bound together in such a way that they are not in simple opposition to each other. Hence it provides the model for the thinking that attempts to retain the experience of a lack as lacking.

Although Heidegger's word *experience* can no more be explicated in terms of familiar experiences than can Hegel's, it is nevertheless worth recalling that experiences of a loss that retain the loss while at the same time showing themselves as a granting are known to us. It can happen that in the absence of someone we experience the depth of our love for them and thus enter into a relation not bound by presence. Mystics have found God in the dark night of the soul and it is now almost commonplace among theologians to recognize the experience of the loss of God in a secular society as an experience of God. Such experiences do not reestablish presence in the midst of absence. They break with the dichotomy of presence and absence, establishing absence as present precisely in its absence.

But what then is the relation between "experience" and the metaphysics of presence? As we have seen, Heidegger is not oblivious to the relation between experiencing and presencing in Hegel. There is no more a question of him adopting the word in the sense it has for Hegel than there is of him rejecting it. Remembrance takes place only on the basis of the experience of the oblivion of Being; this experience marks both a break with metaphysics and a transformation of the meaning of *experience*. The recognition of Hegel's word *experience* as an address of the truth of Being means that there is heard in it the echo of a holding back or withdrawal.

The difference between Hegel's concept of experience and Heidegger's is that the former is tied to the rule of presencing and the latter commemorates it. Phenomenology for Hegel is a *parousia*, whereas for Heidegger it is letting the nonapparent appear as nonapparent. So Heidegger's word *Erfahrung* is not set up in opposition to Hegel's, but, in his remembrance of Hegel's concept of experience as a presencing, he lets the oblivion of Being appear within it as the unsaid in what is said. With his concept of experience, Hegel had sought to obliterate all trace of a lack; the inadequacy that gives rise to the new object gives way. But Heidegger emphasizes that Hegel understands that inadequacy and its overcoming through experience in terms of subject and object; and subjectness is a particular destiny whereby Being withdraws. In an all too brief passage, Heidegger relates Hegel to the essence of technology by way of the epoch of subjectness.[9] In the phrase of the essay, "The Question concerning Technology," we might say that Hegel remains under the grip of "the final delusion."

That Hegel came too early for the final delusion to be experienced as such is not an objection to Hegel's history of philosophy; it belongs to its very nature that it should be the case. Again, if Hegel accords to remembrance a privileged standpoint, that too is not a critical error, but a necessary aspect of the final delusion. Heidegger's remembrance does not have the status of a privileged standpoint. In saying the unsaid, Heidegger does not succeed in saying what previous thinkers had *failed* to say; to say the unsaid is to engage in a "saying not-saying."

For Hegel, the new object and thus the experience of it arises through a reversal or inversion *(Umkehrung)* of consciousness (PS 61; tr. 55). The fundamental experience of Heidegger's thinking is the turn *(Kehre)* from metaphysics to *Ereignis*; it is the entry *(Einkehr)* into *Ereignis*. As experience in Hegel is always to be understood as for "us," the observers, experience in Heidegger is for the thinkers of another beginning who step back into the essence of metaphysics. The experience of the history of thinking is the experience of a lack. Whereas Hegel seeks to make good that lack by completing what each thinker within the history of philosophy has thought and so raise it to the absolute standpoint, Heidegger attempts to hear the lack as a lack and so preserve himself in the experience of the oblivion of Being. To retain the experience of the oblivion of Being is not the same as to retain the oblivion of Being; it is to pass beyond Being into a landscape in which our heritage and thus also our relation to our fundamental categories is transformed.

2. *Ereignis* and the Overcoming of Metaphysics

Ereignis is the fundamental word of Heidegger's later thinking. In ordinary German it customarily means "event." In Heidegger it has another meaning and is usually translated "appropriation." Heidegger himself has said that it can "no more be translated than the Greek *logos* or the Chinese *Tao*" (ID 25; tr. 36). I shall therefore leave it untranslated.

Heidegger is clear that our access to *Ereignis* is not through proof, but through experience (SD 57; TB 53). *Ereignis* is experienced in the essence of modern technology, but as that which brings about the recovery of the world from out of the dominance of technology (ID 25; tr. 37). So technology is a prelude to *Ereignis*. The culmination of the essay "The Question concerning Technology" was the quotation from Hölderlin's poem *Patmos*:

> But where danger is, grows
> The saving power also.[10]

An earlier essay, "The Anaximander Fragment," clarifies the sense of "danger." "Rescue *(Rettung)* comes when and only when danger *is*. Danger is when Being itself advances to its farthest extreme, and when the oblivion that issues from Being itself undergoes reversal" (H 343; EGT 58). A note in Heidegger's own copy confirms that these sentences are concerned with the passage from the essence of technology to *Ereignis*.[11] The experience *(Erfahrung)* of technology reveals technology as the danger *(Gefahr)*. The words *Gefahr* and *Erfahrung* both bear the root *fahren* suggesting a journey. It is the journey of the *Kehre* in which there is a bringing before the eyes *(Augen)* of what was previously concealed.

Heidegger invites us to read the word *Eräugnis* alongside *Ereignis* so that the sense in which it takes place as an insight is apparent.[12] But this does not mean that it is to be understood simply as a power of revelation. Heidegger has not become a victim of the urge to bring everything into the light so that it can be made subject to examination. *Ereignis* also bears within itself its own withdrawal, which Heidegger announces with the word *Enteignis* and which he associates with the *lethe* of *a-letheia* (SD 44; TB 41). The oblivion of Being is not dissolved when it undergoes reversal and insofar as an awakening from the oblivion of Being takes place, it is a being awakened to the oblivion of Being (SD 32; TB 30). In other words, the penetration of the oblivion of Being in remembrance takes place in another withdrawal of Being: "Being, by coming to view as *Ereignis*, disappears as Being" (SD 46; TB 43).

It is essential to recognize that *Ereignis* is not a word for Being (SD 44; TB 40–41). *Ereignis* is the word that arises from the experience of *the lack of a word* for Being. That experience itself gives rise to the insight into the history of metaphysics as a naming of Being. Within metaphysics, Being went unheeded; the words of Being were not recognized as such. Being can thus be thought in terms of *Ereignis*, but not vice versa (US 260 n; WL 129 n). The transformations within the history of Being may, from one perspective, be regarded as quite different from the transformation from Being to *Ereignis*, but insofar as the former are recognized as such only with the transformation of Being into *Ereignis*, they share in *Ereignis*. That is the sense in which "the words of Being" of metaphysics exceed metaphysics and are not bound by its supposed "unity." Within metaphysics, the voice of Being held sway, but was concealed. With the entry into *Ereignis*, the truth of Being appears within the history of metaphysics, but no longer prevails as it once did.

This may be illustrated from the studies of Heidegger's readings of poetic and philosophical language offered above. *Logos* names the Being of language and yet the Being of language always withheld itself from metaphysical thinking. Then, in his lectures on George's poem *Das Wort*, the word *logos* arises as the word that, for commemorative thinking *(Andenken)*, corresponds to what George experienced and retained in renunciation. *Logos* as a word for Being and for the Being of language arises only for a saying that has renounced that speaking by which things were nominated to their Being. It is the fate of the words of Being that they speak as words of Being only in the ringing of stillness *(Geläut der Stille)*. They resound only in their withdrawal.

It is the same with the word *aletheia*. When Heidegger refers the tautological saying "Das Ereignis ereignet" to "the oldest of the old" in Western thought, he is referring to 'that ancient something that conceals itself in *a-letheia*' (SD 25; TB 24). What conceals itself in *aletheia*, as a trace, is *lethe*, concealment. *Lethe* is the heart of *aletheia* and only at the end of philosophy does this word, which stands at the beginning, open its heart (SD 78; TB 71). Only at the end of the history of Being does the oblivion of Being announce itself. "Now this concealment does not conceal itself..." (SD 44; TB 41). What takes place is not the overcoming of a falsity, a *pseudos*; for the opposition between truth and falsity is itself metaphysical. What emerges is not the ground that underlies metaphysics; for how could concealment serve as a ground? Nor when we hear the *lethe* of *a-letheia* is a new order being established. We are instead witnessing a transformation of language that, because language always stands in a relation to previous language, cannot simply turn its back on what has gone before. The transformation of language is a passage into a "saying not-saying" (ID 66; tr. 73). This does not mean only a passage away from the priority accorded to the assertion. The "not" of "not-saying" is the "not" of the lack of a word of Being in the way in which it permeates all language. *A-letheia* says "unconcealment," but at the same time says this pervasive concealment.

We cannot say that *Ereignis* is a word of Being, but we can say that it is the word of the overcoming of metaphysics, so long as we do not fall into the common misunderstandings of what *overcoming* means. It would be a cause for some surprise if, in publications spanning more than fifty years, everything that Heidegger says about the relation between his thinking and that of metaphysics was perfectly uniform. It took him many years to recognize the experience of the oblivion of Being as an experience of the lack of the word of Being marking both the fulfillment of metaphysics and at the same time the entry into another beginning. In *Being and Time*, the experience has not yet been recognized as granting the insight into the history of Being; many of the concepts of *Being and Time* had subsequently to be rethought in this light (NII 415; EP 14-15).

Nevertheless there is a clear continuity in Heidegger's relation to metaphysics and it is reflected in a similarity between the formulas that at different times he has used to describe that relation. There are three phrases, each belonging to a different period, but they share the same provocative tone that has proved a source of confusion to Heidegger's commentators.

In *Being and Time*, the phrase was "the task of destroying the history of ontology." The work to be done was not as negative as the phrase made it sound. The destruction as something negative was directed against the attitudes current in historical investigation of philosophy at that time, whether problem-oriented or belonging to the history of ideas. The destruction as something positive was directed toward uncovering the original experiences that have since governed the tradition, but our access to which had been blocked by that tradition. This was well illustrated later in the book when the results of the phenomenological investigation of truth were found to coincide with the historical investigation of the Greek word *aletheia*. "The proposed 'definition' of truth is not a *shaking off* of the tradition, but a more original appropriation *(Aneignung)* of it" (SZ 220; tr. 262). The task here described as *Aneignung* is a clear anticipation of the destiny later called *Ereignis* (ID 24-25; tr. 36).[13]

With the insight into the history of Being, which was absent from *Being and Time*, the term *destruction* gave way. The preferred term was now "the overcoming *(Überwindung)* of metaphysics," which again has negative connotations reinforced by its use as a title by Carnap for a famous attack on Heidegger's "What is Metaphysics?"[14] Again the negative connotations are misleading, a point Heidegger makes with the introduction of the word *Verwindung*, which addresses the issue of the oblivion of Being as oblivion (VA 78-79; EP 91-92). The task is not to dismiss metaphysics, but to come to terms with it. We cannot simply abandon metaphysics by ignoring it, which would be a way of allowing it to be perpetuated. With the notion of "overcoming metaphysics," the relation between the return to the first beginning of Western thinking, on the one hand, and the end of philosophy, on the other, was more clearly articulated. This is reflected, for example, in the way that the "original experiences" that were the focus of the "destruction" came to be thought more as traces. What above all differentiates the "destruction" from the "overcoming of metaphysics" is that the latter thinks more resolutely the experience that made the former possible — the end of philosophy as another beginning.

In the 1962 essay "Time and Being," a phrase appears that seems at first sight to mark a striking change in Heidegger's relation to metaphysics. It runs:

> To think Being without regard to beings means to think Being without regard to metaphysics. Yet a regard for metaphysics still prevails even in the intention to overcome metaphysics. Therefore our task is to cease all overcoming, and leave metaphysics to itself. (SD 25; TB 24)

Does this mean that the ending of metaphysics, which according to an earlier essay was supposed to last "longer than the previous history of metaphysics" (VA 71; EP 85), was over after a couple of decades? In the report of a seminar on "Time and Being," Heidegger explicated these sentences further. To think Being without beings does not mean to disregard the relation to beings as inessential to Being. It means that Being is not to be thought in the manner of metaphysics, either in terms of the *summum ens* as *causa sui* or in terms of the ontological difference whereby Being is conceived of as being for the sake of beings (SD 35-36; TB 33). The explication is not as striking as the original phrase. Indeed the explication says nothing that Heidegger had not frequently said earlier. We might conclude that Heidegger's remarks against the program of "overcoming metaphysics" are directed, not so much against his own earlier attempts, as against those commentators who had still not seen the radical difference between metaphysical thinking and the thinking that steps back into it as *Verwindung*. If there is a division at all — and my qualifications will appear in the next section — it is between the period of the destruction and that of the overcoming of metaphysics. There is no third phase in relation to this issue.

Nevertheless there is something more to the phrase "leave metaphysics to itself" than is indicated by the notion of "overcoming metaphysics," although here again we find, not a completely new development in Heidegger's thinking, but the culmination of a long development. Heidegger was directing his remarks not only against a certain interpretation of a program, but against all ideas that the overcoming of metaphysics was a program carried out by our own efforts. That overcoming should abate *(ablassen)* and that metaphysics should be left *(überlassen)* to itself both point to releasement *(Gelassenheit)*. The emphasis is on the fact that entry into *Ereignis* is not our own doing. Nor is releasement. *Ereignis* appropriates human beings to releasement (US 261; WL 130). Hence *Ereignis* is at work in George's poem *Das Wort*, for the sorrow of the renouncing poet is explicated by Heidegger as releasement (US 169; WL 66).

Far from it being the case that in this later period Heidegger distances himself from the task of constantly returning to the history of previous thinking, Heidegger reiterates his constant concern that "only when we turn thoughtfully toward what has already been thought, will we be turned to use for what must still be thought" (ID 30; tr. 41).

3. *Ereignis* and the Transformation of Language

The relation between the poet's experience of the holy and the thinker's insight into the truth of Being is attested to in the *Letter on Humanism*:

> The holy, which alone is the essential sphere of divinity, which in turn alone affords a dimension for the gods and for God, comes to radiate only when Being itself beforehand and after extensive preparation has been illuminated and is experienced in its truth. (W 169; BW 218)

The parallel between the experience of the poet Hölderlin and his own experience as a thinker is crucial to Heidegger's thought of "another beginning" *(der andere Anfang).*[15] Both experiences arise initially as a default. For the poet, it is the departure of the gods; for the thinker, it is the failure of the truth of Being to arrive. Heidegger understands both these experiences as experiences of language.

On Heidegger's reading, Hölderlin had been granted a privileged insight into the poetic vocation of naming the gods, precisely at the time when it seemed that the poet's vocation could no longer be fulfilled. Through the experience of the lack of the gods, it was given to Hölderlin to name the hitherto unknown realm that dictated the names of the gods: "And what I saw, may the holy be my word." Heidegger, in part through the insight won by his reading of Hölderlin, came to understand his own experience of thinking as the experience of the lack of a word for Being. This lack introduced him to the truth of Being as it took place within metaphysics and to *Ereignis* as that which grants the truth of Being. *Ereignis* is the word of the thinker of thinking, as Hölderlin's word *the holy* was the word of the poet of poetry.

In recalling the vocation of poet and thinker, Hölderlin and Heidegger were not merely looking to the past. They were the messengers of another beginning arising out of the first. Their insight into it was not formed on the basis of an experience that had won them a self-awareness about their respective tasks that had hitherto been lacking to them. The experience of the disruption of their vocations was not one that raised them to a higher level of self-consciousness on a Hegelian model. They had not won greater control of their destiny. On the contrary, they were left more aware of their dependence on destiny.

This was most apparent in the transformed relation to language summarized by the sentence, "Man speaks only insofar as he corresponds to language" (US 33; PLT 210). This corresponding *(Entsprechen)* was itself a speaking

(Sprechen), but a speaking that took place after listening to language, a *Nachsprechen*. Thus the discussion of saying as owning *(Eignen)* does not point to man having a greater control over language, as if he had in *Ereignis* inherited it as a possession (US 258; WL 127). We dwell in *Ereignis* only insofar as we are appropriated *(vereignet)* by language (US 266; WL 134). The transformation of language here announced is therefore necessarily a transformation of humankind from out of mastery into submission (ID 25; tr. 37). The view that language was an instrument broke down with the break in the succession of words of Being.

For the poet Hölderlin, the words *hymn* and *song* serve to announce the transformed language of another beginning of another history. Heidegger says of the word *hymn* that it is the *Ereignis* of the holy (ED 74). *Hymn* is the word of a transformation of language compelled by the holy, in which the holy—by being named—enters into its own (ED 187ff.). In 1954 the manuscript of the final version of Hölderlin's hymn "Celebration of Peace" *(Friedensfeier)* was discovered. It contained the lines:

Viel hat von Morgen an,
Seit ein Gespräch wir sind und hören voneinander,
Erfahren der Mensch; bald sind aber Gesang (wir).

Much, from the morning onwards,
Since we have been a dialogue and have heard from one another,
Has man experienced; but soon we shall be song.[16]

Quoting these lines in the lecture "The Essence of Language" in order to clarify how he understands the transformation of language that takes place through *Ereignis*, Heidegger identifies the dialogue *(Gespräch)* of the poem as that dialogue between men and gods that is mediated by the poet. He does not understand the song as a rejection of dialogue as its contrary; he emphasizes the kinship between them. "Song remains dialogue." He says of song that it is "the celebration of the advent of the gods—in which advent everything falls silent" (US 182; WL 78). The silence of the lack of a name for the gods does not pass away with the advent of the coming gods; song echoes with silence. Nietzsche's *Singen* in *Also sprach Zarathustra* and George's poem *Das Wort*, which belongs in a group of poems under the heading *Das Lied*, are also song.

Like song, Heidegger's "saying not-saying" speaks from silence. This silence is the silence of the experience that grants the entry into *Ereignis* and the passage from the dominance of Being as presencing. In "The Way to Language" Heidegger says of *Ereignis* both that it is experienced in the essence of technology (US 263; WL 131), and that it is *only* experienced as the abiding gift yielded by saying (US 258; WL 127). There is no contradiction here; technology is the completion of metaphysics in which the transformation of language takes place. "Do we see the lightning flash of Being in the essence of technology? The flash that comes out of silence, as silence itself? Silence stills."[17] The transformed language is not the contrary of metaphysical language, any more than song is the contrary of dialogue in the quotation from Hölderlin. In response to the question as to whether metaphysical names can be used outside metaphysics, Heidegger insists that metaphysical language can become a nonmetaphysical language without any change in its expressions (VS 87-88). Whether Heidegger on that occasion raised the difficulties inherent in the phrase "beyond metaphysics" is not recorded. That, according to his view, metaphysical language already speaks "non-metaphysically" when certain words of the thinkers of metaphysics are recognized through remembrance as words of Being, should be clear from the earlier chapters. But the nonmetaphysical does not oppose itself to the metaphysical; nor does the metaphysical cease with the advent of the nonmetaphysical, not least because it needs the metaphysical.

The relation between the Greek language, which is the source of all metaphysical language, and the German language, whose resources he always seemed to be stretching, had, Heidegger found, already been an issue for Hölderlin, most notably in a letter written to Böhlendorff in December of 1801.[18] The question concerning these two languages goes far beyond issues of terminology. For Hölderlin, the advent and nearness of the gods is proper *(Eigene)* to the Greeks, but to appropriate *(aneignen)* it they must pass through what is foreign to them: the clarity of presentation. For the Germans, the clarity of presentation is what is proper to them and through the foreignness of "the fire in heaven," they enter into the appropriation *(Aneignung)* and use *(Gebrauch)* of that which is their own (ED 83-84). Metaphysics is, in the same way, a foreign land for Heidegger in his passage toward a site other than metaphysics, which, to evoke the silence, he leaves nameless (US 138; WL 42). And yet, although Heidegger characterizes the transformation of thinking as the passage from the site of metaphysics to the unnamed site, the thinkers of another beginning need to maintain remembrance of what is foreign to them.

Hölderlin develops his account of the relation of the Greeks and the Germans in another letter to his friend Böhlendorff, this one in the autumn of 1802, after his return from Bordeaux. The letter begins: "Dear friend! I think that we shall not comment upon the poets before our time, but that the mode of song will take on a different character...."[19] Heidegger uses this passage to explore the sense in which his own thinking is provisional *(Vorläufigkeit)* (SD 41; TB 38). The word *provisional* does not mean only that Heidegger's thinking is preparatory *(vorbereitend)*, but that it is, through the step back into the essence of metaphysics, anticipatory. There is also a provisional character to Heidegger's thinking that I have not always done justice to here; it expresses itself—particularly in respect of the overcoming of technology—in the uncertainty of another beginning. The thinking of the turning is not based on calculation, but then no more is the uncertainty that accompanies it. But the primary sense in which Heidegger's thinking is provisional is none of these. Heidegger's thinking is provisional in that its language is provisional. *Being*, for example, is only a provisional word (VA 229: EGT 78). It is ambiguous in the sense described earlier, whereby it both belongs and does not belong to metaphysics. Insofar as most of Heidegger's lectures and essays were devoted to "Being" those works remain provisional. This is not to cast doubt on them, but to let them be heard as anticipatory. Hence Heidegger's motto for the complete edition of his essays and lectures, now in the course of publication, is "Wege—nicht Werke," "Paths—not works."[20]

We should not underestimate the difficulty this poses. Heidegger had in the Introduction to *Being and Time* already recognized the way in which the propositional form served as an obstacle: "It is possible for every phenomenological concept and sentence drawn from original sources to degenerate when communicated as an assertion" (SZ 36; tr. 60–61). The characterization of sentences as assertions and the predominance accorded to them was, for Heidegger, a consequence of the predominance of truth in the sense of correctness. Phenomenology, as the investigation of what is hidden as hidden, rejects the way of objectification and hence the mode of speech that conforms to it. Heidegger, in his later essays, continues to seek ways of disturbing the tendency to think in assertions. In one place he warns us that what he says will be misunderstood if taken as a series of assertions and invites us to attend to the path of thinking rather than its content (ID 9; tr. 23). Heidegger's way with language is akin to that of negative theology insofar as it speaks by denial and renunciation (SD 51; TB 47). It is, however, much more than this. The "saying not-saying" cannot be reduced to the assertion and negation of one and the same proposition in quick succession. It is an invitation to a certain kind of reading where we hear first the metaphysical at work throughout language and then in a second reading the silence, the concealment, that resounds in it.

Just as there is a double play involved in Heidegger's own readings, which I have attempted to show at work in his readings of Plato and George, it is also necessary to provide a double reading of Heidegger. Heidegger exercises it on his own work when he rereads his own essays. This is particularly the case when it comes to rereading the earlier works in the light of the insight into the history of Being. No essay better illustrates this than the lecture "What is Metaphysics?" and the reinterpretation it undergoes in the Postscript and Introduction subsequently added to it. Unfortunately, these reinterpretations have tended to be reduced to the level of self-correction. So the question has been raised as to whether Heidegger I is indeed an improvement on Heidegger II.

The dangers of the formulation "Heidegger I and II" arise when it is allowed to serve as a characterization of different periods of Heidegger's career as a thinker. Many of the objections against the so-called turning from Heidegger I to

Heidegger II have taken the form of attempts to multiply the periods of Heidegger's development, so we have been offered Heidegger III, and even IV. It is no better when the attempt is made to suggest that Heidegger's thinking has been uniform throughout. The "philosophical" issue here is not a question of intellectual history, but the question of the relation between the thinking that takes place within the insight into the history of Being and that which is "without" it. Or, better said, the question concerns their "right" to be recognized as the only alternatives. Heidegger's own comment on the division should always be borne in mind: "Only by way of what Heidegger I has thought does one gain access to what is to-be-thought by Heidegger II."[21] What Heidegger says about the relation between Heidegger I and Heidegger II is the same as what he says about the relation between "the essence of truth" and "the truth of essence"; the apparent order is to be reversed so that now the former arises from the latter and generally that which is prima facie earlier is preceded by what comes later. But then again, the later does not have an absolute priority over the earlier; Heidegger II precedes Heidegger I only as a trace and it should be acknowledged that some readers of Heidegger appear to have already recognized this.[22]

The mutual dependency of Heidegger I and II ensures that same ambiguity in Heidegger's saying not-saying as may be found in all metaphysical language when read at the end of philosophy. And that ambiguity is also at play in Heidegger when it is not a question of the passage between two texts from different periods. As was seen in the previous chapter, a word like *non-essence* can within a single text say, by renunciation, what cannot be said in the language of metaphysics. And yet this renunciation is not something we do, but a provision of our relation to metaphysics, thus inviting the reflection that there were indeed two texts: one is the text of metaphysics, while the other is, in one of Heidegger's best formulations, left "without a name" (US 138; WL 42).

All of this, however, presents an insurmountable barrier to the commentator, particularly insofar as he is supposed to provide an answer to the question: *what* does Heidegger say? One cannot readily say *what* Heidegger says for the simple reason that Heidegger overcomes the "what" of *essentia* by transforming the way of saying. Hence all writing about Heidegger should begin and end with a disclaimer. The disclaimer, in attempting to be faithful to what claimed Heidegger, must at the same time disregard his warnings and lift the silence about silence. In a dialogue with a Japanese professor, Heidegger did not demur from his partner's judgement that "to talk and write about silence is what produces the most obnoxious chatter" except to ask "who could simply be silent of silence?" (US 152; WL 52). Silence before silence is essential to hear the lack of the word of Being as a lack, and not to conceal it, as mindless talk could conceal anxiety. Yet Heidegger kept silent in a different way from simply refraining from speaking or publishing, as is clear from the many eloquent volumes that are his legacy to us. He entertained a speech that maintained a *telling* silence by speaking from that silence and seeking to preserve it. The experience of the silence arising from the lack of a word for Being, does not, for Heidegger, mark an end, but the entry into a language that speaks from the break in language. For a commentary on Heidegger to try to imitate Heidegger's transformed language would be to render commentary pointless. The task for the moment is to try to learn to read Heidegger so that the silence is not dissolved. It is liable to become more difficult as talk about the "ringing of stillness" and "the saying not-saying" becomes more commonplace.

There is no shortage, in Heidegger's own writings, of disclaimers of the kind that are so tempting for commentators on Heidegger. One of the most striking arises at the close of the lecture "Time and Being", which ends simply with the words "The lecture has spoken merely in propositional statements" (SD 25; TB 24). In a seminar on the lecture the comment was explained as follows: "The lecture's risk lies in the fact that it speaks in propositional statements about something essentially incommensurable with this kind of saying" (SD 27; TB 25). But Heidegger knew of another way with language, a way which is the destiny of that thinking whose task is to think at the time of the lack of a word of Being. It would be hard to improve upon the description Heidegger gives of it at the end of his 1937 lectures under the title *The Eternal Recurrence of the Same*.

> Supremely thoughtful utterance does not consist simply in growing taciturn when it is a matter of saying what is properly to be said; it consists in saying the matter in such a way that it is named in nonsaying. The utterance of thinking is a telling silence. Such utterance corresponds to the most profound essence of language, which has its origin in silence. (NI 471-72)[23]

And what of the reading that corresponds to such thinking? Will metaphysics continue to be read only as a series of propositional statements? Or have we not entered into an epoch when to reread the propositional statements that appear to constitute the site of the tradition is to entertain a language whose words have already broken and — to recall the words of Eliot that serve as the epigraph for my essay — will not stay in place?

NOTES

1. H-G. Gadamer, *Wahrheit und Methode* (Tübingen: J. C. B. Mohr, 1972), pp. 64–65; trans. W. Glen-Doepel, *Truth and Method* (London: Sheed & Ward, 1975, and New York: Seabury, 1976), pp. 61–62.

2. G. Simmel, "Das Abenteuer," *Philosophische Kultur: Gesammelte Essays* (Leipzig: W. Klinkhardt, 1911), pp. 11–28; trans. David Kettler, "The Adventurer," *On Individuality*

and Social Forms, ed. D. N. Levine (Chicago: University of Chicago Press, 1971), pp. 187-98.

3. I borrow the phrase from T. S. Eliot's "Journey of the Magi," *Collected Poems 1909-62* (London: Faber & Faber, 1963), p. 110.

4. The essay arose out of a seminar held at Freiburg during the summer semester of 1942 and the winter semester 1942-43. It was first published in 1950.

5. A survey of the different interpretations can be found in K. R. Dove, "Hegel's Phenomenological Method," *Review of Metaphysics* 23, no. 4 (1970):615-41.

6. *Holzwege*, p. 184-85; trans. *Hegel's Concept of Experience*, p. 141-44. See also "Ursprünglicher Zwischentitel," *Phänomenologie des Geistes*, Gesammelte Werke Band 9 (Hamburg: Felix Meiner, 1980), pp. 469-71.

7. Heidegger says that the word *experience* recedes "in the last of the main sections which presents the appearance of consciousness as Spirit" (*Holzwege*, p. 184; trans. *Hegel's Concept of Experience*, pp. 143-44). The word appears at the beginning of the chapter on Spirit, "Spirit that is certain of itself. Morality." It does not appear in the crucial discussion of "Evil and its Forgiveness." The word is strikingly absent from the chapter on Religion, except for one important appearance at *Phänomenologie des Geistes*, p. 380; trans. A. V. Miller *Phenomenology of Spirit*, p. 429, and two occurrences of the verb in the last section of chapter seven.

8. See chapter 1, section 2 above.

9. "It is, to be sure, an altogether different question whether and in what way subjectness is a peculiar destiny in the essence of Being, whereby the unconcealedness of Being (not the truth of particular beings) *withdraws*, thus determining an epoch of its own." *Holzwege*, p. 176; trans. *Hegel's Concept of Experience*, p. 131-32.

10. "Wo aber Gefahr ist, wächst/Das Rettende auch."

11. "Das Gestell als äusserste Vergessenheit und zugleich als Wink in das Ereignis." *Holzwege*, Gesamtausgabe Band 5 (Frankfurt: Klostermann, 1977), p. 373.

12. *Die Technik und die Kehre* (Pfullingen: Neske, 1962), p. 44; trans. W. Lovitt, *The Question concerning Technology*, p. 45. It should also be noted that the word *insight*, which has frequently appeared in this study, receives its authorization from this lecture, which was one of a series called *Einblick in das was ist*.

13. The words *Destruktion* and *Aneignung* may already be found in the unpublished essay "Anmerkungen zu Karl Jaspers 'Psychologie der Weltanschauungen,'" dating from 1919-21. For example, *Wegmarken*, Gesamtausgabe Band 9 (Frankfurt: Klostermann, 1976), pp. 34-35.

14. The title of Carnap's essay was "Überwindung der Metaphysik durch logische Analyse der Sprache" (*Erkenntnis* 2 [1931]). Heidegger's essay entitled "Überwindung der Metaphysik" is a collection of notes from the years 1936 to 1946. In a 1927 lecture course we find the sentence "This overcoming of Hegel is the intrinsically necessary step in the development of Western philosophy which must be made for it to remain at all alive." Although Heidegger here uses the word *Überwindung*, the passage is striking insofar as it not only omits reference to the "end of philosophy," but even seems to exclude it. *Die Grundprobleme der Phänomenologie* (Frankfurt: Klostermann, 1927), p. 254; trans. A. Hofstadter, *The Basic Problems of Phenomenology* (Bloomington, Ind.: Indiana University Press, 1982), p. 178. This suggests that the remarks about the end of philosophy from the same lecture series (quoted in chapter 1, section 3 above) must be read with caution.

15. There are at least nine occurrences of the phrase in Heidegger's published works; the first of these is in the 1935 lecture course, *Einführung in die Metaphysik* (Tübingen: Niemeyer, 1966), p. 29; trans. R. Manheim, *An Introduction to Metaphysics* (New Haven, Conn.: Yale University Press, 1973), p. 39. The phrase arises particularly in the context of the discussion of Nietzsche. Heidegger's avoidance of the phrase "new beginning" is important for showing his sensitivity to the suggestion that a completely new start outside the sphere of influence of previous thinking is possible. "Another beginning" is only possible in remembrance of the first beginning. The theme of "another beginning" has been taken up in the work of Werner Marx and, more recently, Petra Jaeger and Heribert Boeder.

16. *Unterwegs zur Sprache*, pp. 182 and 266; trans. *On the Way to Language*, pp. 78 and 135. The translation of the poem (with minor changes) by Michael Hamburger, *Friedrich Hölderlin: Poems and Extracts* (London: Routledge & Kegan Paul, and Ann Arbor, Mich.: University of Michigan Press, 1966), p. 439.

17. "Die Stille stillt," *Die Technik und die Kehre*, p. 47; trans. *The Question concerning Technology*, p. 49.

18. Quoted by Heidegger in *Erläuterungen zu Hölderlins Dichtung*, zweite Auflage, 1951, p. 83. A translation of the letter, and that mentioned in note 19, may be found in *The Poet's Vocation: Selections from the letters of Hölderlin, Rimbaud and Hart Crane*, ed. W. Burford and C. Middleton (Austin, Texas: University of Texas Press, no date).

19. Quoted by Heidegger in *Erläuterungen zu Hölderlins Dichtung*, vierte Auflage, 1971, pp. 157-59.

20. *Frühe Schriften*, Gesamtausgabe Band 1 (Frankfurt: Klostermann, 1978), p. 437.

21. "Brief an P. William J. Richardson," W. J. Richardson, *Heidegger. Through Phenomenology to Thought* (The Hague: Nijhoff, 1963), pp. xxiif.

22. For example, J. Sallis "Into the Clearing," *Heidegger. The Man and the Thinker*, ed. T. Sheehan (Chicago: Precedent, 1981), p. 107: "Here it is a matter not simply of change *from* the text *Being and Time*, but rather of an immanent, i.e. radicalizing critique set upon bringing into the open something already in play, inconspicuously, perhaps even concealedly, in *Being and Time* itself."

23. The translation is by David Krell and it has appeared in *Boundary 2* 9, no. 3/10, no. 1 (1981), p. 38. It is drawn from *Nietzsche II: The Eternal Recurrence of the Same* (New York: Harper & Row, forthcoming).

Bibliography

Professor Hans-Martin Sass gives a complete listing of Heidegger's published writings as well as translations in his *Martin Heidegger: Bibliography and Glossary* Bowling Green State University, Ohio, Philosophy Documentation Center, 1982. He also lists—the number is not exact because there are some errors in the numbering—5632 books and essays on Heidegger. I have therefore decided to confine my bibliography to a selection of the secondary writings that I can recommend to anyone wishing to pursue further the themes of this book. Because the following list is a highly selective one, some items that are mentioned in the notes above are not listed here.

Allemann, B. *Hölderlin und Heidegger*. Freiburg: Atlantis, 1954.

Arendt, H. "Heidegger's Will-not-to-Will." In *The Life of the Mind*, vol. 2. New York: Harcourt Brace Jovanovich, 1978.

Ballard, E. G., and Scott, C. E., eds. *Martin Heidegger in Europe and America*. The Hague: Nijhoff, 1973.

Beaufret, J. *Introduction aux Philosophies de l'Existence*. Paris: Denoël, 1971.

——. *Dialogue avec Heidegger*. 1, Philosophie grecque; 2, Philosophie Moderne; 3, Approche de Heidegger. Paris: Minuit, 1973-74.

Blanchot, M. "La parole 'sacrée' de Hölderlin." *La Part du Feu*. Paris: Gallimard, 1949.

——. "L' itinéraire de Hölderlin." In *L'espace littéraire*, pp. 367-89. Paris: Gallimard, 1978. Translated by A. Smock as 'Hölderlin's Itinerary.' *The Space of Literature*, pp. 269-76. Lincoln, Neb.: Univ. of Nebraska Press, 1982.

Biemel, W. *Martin Heidegger in Selbstzeugnissen und Bilddokumentum*. Hamburg: Rowohlt, 1973. Translated by J. L. Mehta as *Martin Heidegger. An Illustrated Study*. New York: Harcourt Brace Jovanovich, and London: Routledge & Kegan Paul, 1976.

——. "Heideggers Deutung des Heiligen bei Hölderlin." *Theologische Forschung* 58 (1976):181-90.

Birault, H. *Heidegger et l'expérience de la pensée*. Paris: Gallimard, 1978.

Boeder, H. "Der Verschiedene im 'anderen Anfang.'" *Der Idealismus und seine Gegenwart*. Festschrift für Werner Marx zum 65. Geburtstag, pp. 3-35. Hrsg. U. Guzzoni, B. Rang und L. Siep. Hamburg: Felix Meiner, 1976.

Brogan, W. *Nature and Man: A Commentary on Heidegger's Interpretation of Aristotle's Physics B.1*. Ph.D. dissertation, Duquesne University. Ann Arbor, Mich.: University Microfilms International, 1981.

Buddeburg, Else. *Heidegger und die Dichtung*. Stuttgart: J. B. Metzler, 1953.

Caputo, J. D. *The Mystical Element in Heidegger's Thought*. Athens, Ohio: Ohio Univ. Press, 1978.

——. *Heidegger and Aquinas*. New York: Fordham University Press, 1982.

De Man, P. "Les exégèses de Hölderlin par Martin Heidegger." *Critique* 11-13 (1955):800-819. Translated by W. Godzich as "Heidegger's Exegeses of Hölderlin." *Blindness and Insight*, pp. 246-66. Minneapolis: University of Minnesota Press; London: Methuen, 1983.

Derrida, J. *L'écriture et la différence*. Paris: Seuil, 1967. Translated by A. Bass as *Writing and Difference*. London: Routledge & Kegan Paul; Chicago: Univ. of Chicago Press, 1978.

——. "Le retrait de la métaphore." *Po&sie*, Autumn 1978, pp. 103-26. Translated as "The *retrait* of metaphor." *Enclitic* 2 (1978): 5-33.

——. *Marges de la philosophie*. Paris: Minuit, 1972. Translated by A. Bass as *Margins of Philosophy*. Chicago: Univ. of Chicago Press, 1982.

Elliston, F., ed. *Heidegger's Existential Analytic*. The Hague: Mouton, 1978.

Emad, P. *Heidegger and the Phenomenology of Values*. Glen Ellyn: Torey, 1981.

——. "Technology as Presence: Heidegger's View." *Listening* 16, no. 2 (1981): 133-44.

——. "Heidegger on Pain." *Zeitschrift für Philosophische Forschung*, Band 36, no. 3 (1982):345-60.

Exercices de la patience no. 3/4. Paris: Obsidiane, 1982.

Feick, H. *Index zu Heideggers "Sein und Zeit"* 3. Auflage, Tübingen: Niemeyer, 1980.

Frings, M. S., ed. *Heidegger and the Quest for Truth*. Chicago: Quadrangle, 1968.

Gadamer, H-G. "Zur Einführung." *Martin Heidegger: Der Ursprung des Kunstwerkes*, pp. 102-25. Stuttgart: Reclam, 1960. Translated by D. E. Linge as "Heidegger's Later Philosophy" *Philosophical Hermeneutics*, pp. 213-28. Berkeley, Calif.: Univ. of California Press, 1976.

——. *Kleine Schriften*, vols 1-4. Tübingen, J. C. B. Mohr, 1967, 1967, 1972, and 1977.

——. "Hegel und Heidegger." *Hegels Dialektik*, pp. 83-96. Tübingen: J. C. B. Mohr, 1971. Translated by P. Christopher Smith as "Hegel and Heidegger." *Hegel's Dialectic*, pp. 100-116. New Haven, Conn.: Yale Univ. Press, 1976.

——. "The Continuity of History and the Existential Moment." Translated by Thomas Wren. *Philosophy Today* 16 (1972):230-40.

——. *Wahrheit und Methode.* Tübingen: J. C. B. Mohr, 1972. Translated by W. Glen-Doepel as *Truth and Method.* London: Sheed & Ward, 1975; New York: Seabury, 1976.

——. *Philosophical Hermeneutics.* Translated by D. E. Linge. Berkeley, Calif.: Univ. of California Press, 1976.

——. 'Plato und Heidegger' *Der Idealismus und seine Gegenwart. Festschrift für Werner Marx zu 65. Geburtstag.* Hrsg. U. Guzzoni, B. Rang, und L. Siep, pp. 166-75. Hamburg: Felix Meiner, 1976. Translated by I. Sprung as "Plato and Heidegger." *The Question of Being.* Edited by M. Sprung. University Park, Pa.: Pennsylvania State Univ. Press, 1978.

——. "Heidegger's Paths." Translated by C. Kayser and G. Stack. *Philosophical Exchange* 2 (Summer 1979):80-91.

——. *Heideggers Wege.* Tübingen: J. C. B. Mohr, 1983.

Greisch, J. "Les mots et les roses. La métaphore chez Heidegger." *Revue des Sciences Philosophiques et Théologiques* 1 (1973):71-112.

Guzzoni, Ute, ed. *Nachdenken über Heidegger.* Hildesheim: Gerstenberg, 1980.

Haar, M. "La Pensée et le Moi chez Heidegger." *Revue de métaphysique et de morale* 80, no. 4 (1975):456-84.

——. "Heidegger et l'essence de la technique." *Revue de l'Enseignement Philosophique* 30, no. 2 (Décembre 1979-Janvier 1980): 20-34.

——. "Structures hégéliennes dans la pensée heideggérienne de l'Histoire." *Revue de métaphysique et de morale* 85, no. 1 (1980):48-59.

Halliburton, D. *Poetic Thinking. An Approach to Heidegger.* Chicago: Univ. of Chicago Press, 1981.

"Heidegger and the History of Philosophy." *The Monist* 64, no. 4 (October 1981).

Herrmann, Friedrich-Wilhelm von, *Die Selbstinterpretation Martin Heideggers.* Meisenheim am Glan: A. Hain, 1964.

Hyppolite, J. "Étude du commentaire de l'introduction à la Phenomenologie par Heidegger." *Figures de la pensée philosophique,* vol 2, pp. 625-42. Paris: Presses Universitaires, 1971.

Ijsseling, S. "Heidegger and the destruction of ontology" *Man and World* 15 (1982):3-16.

Jaeger, P. *Heideggers Ansatz zur Verwindung der Metaphysik in der Epoche von "Sein und Zeit"* Frankfurt: Peter Lang; Bern: Herbert Lang, 1976.

Janicaud, D. "Heidegger and Method." *Man and World* 9, no. 2 (1976):664-76.

——. "Savoir Philosophique et pensée meditante." *Revue de l'Enseignement Philosophique* 27, no. 3 (1977):1-14.

Janicaud, D., and Matteri, J-F. *La métaphysique à la limite.* Paris, Presses Universitaires de France, 1983.

Kearney, R., and O'Leary, J. S., eds. *Heidegger et la question de Dieu*. Paris: Bernard Grasset, 1980

Klostermann, V., hrsg. *Durchblicke*. Frankfurt: Klostermann, 1970.

Kockelmans, J., ed. *On Heidegger and Language*. Evanston, Ill.: Northwestern Univ. Press, 1972.

Kolb, D. "Review of *Hegels Phänomenologie des Geistes*, hrsg. I. Görland, Heidegger Gesamtausgabe Band 32." *The Owl of Minerva* 13, no. 2 (1982): 3-6.

Krell, D. F. "Nietzsche in Heidegger's 'Kehre.'" *The Southern Journal of Philosophy* 13, no. 2 (1975):197-204.

——. "On the Manifold Meaning of 'Aletheia': Brentano, Aristotle, Heidegger." *Research in Phenomenology* 5 (1975):77-94.

——. "Toward 'Sein und Zeit.' Heidegger's Early Review of Jasper's 'Psychologie der Weltanschauugen.'" *Journal of the British Society for Phenomenology* 6, no. 3 (1975):147-56.

——. "Being and Truth, Being and Time." *Research in Phenomenology* 6 (1976):151-66.

——. "Heidegger, Nietzsche, Hegel." *Nietzsche-Studien* 5 (1976):255-62.

——. "From *Fundamental-* to *Frontalontologie:* A Discussion of Heidegger's Marburg Lectures of 1925-6, 1927 and 1928." *Research in Phenomenology* 10 (1980):208-34.

Krüger, G. "Martin Heidegger und der Humanismus." *Studia Philosophica* 9 (1949):93-129.

Loscerbo, J. *Being and Technology*. The Hague: Nijhoff, 1981.

Macomber, W. B. *The Anatomy of Disillusion: Martin Heidegger's Notion of Truth*. Evanston, Ill.: Northwestern Univ. Press, 1967.

Marx, W. *Heidegger und die Tradition*. Stuttgart: Kohlhammer, 1961. Translated by T. Kisiel and M. Greene as *Heidegger and the Tradition*. Evanston, Ill.: Northwestern Univer. Press, 1971.

——. *Vernunft und Welt*. The Hague: Nijhoff, 1970. Translated by T. Yates and R. Geuss as *Reason and World*. The Hague: Nijhoff, 1971.

Marx, W., ed. *Heidegger: Freiburger Universitätsvorträge zu seinem Gedenken*. Freiburg: Alber, 1977. Translated by S. Davis as *Heidegger Memorial Lectures*. Pittsburgh: Duquesne University, 1982.

McCumber, J. "Language and Appropriation: The Nature of Heideggerian Dialogue." *The Personalist* 60 (1979):384-96.

Mehta, J. L. *Martin Heidegger: The Way and the Vision*. Honolulu: Univ. of Hawaii Press, 1976.

Moser, S. "Toward a Metaphysics of Technology." Translated by W. Carroll. *Philosophy Today* 15 (1971):129-56.

Murray, M. *Modern Philosophy of History*. The Hague: Nijhoff, 1970.

———. "Heidegger's Hermeneutic Reading of Hölderlin: The Signs of Time." *The Eighteenth Century* 21, no. 1 (1980):42-66.

Murray, M., ed. *Heidegger and Modern Philosophy*. New Haven, Conn.: Yale Univ. Press, 1978.

Neske, G. *Erinnerung an Martin Heidegger*. Pfullingen: Neske, 1977.

Orth, E. W., hrsg. *Zeit und Zeitlichkeit bei Husserl und Heidegger*. Phänomenologische Forschung 14. Freiburg: Alber, 1983.

Pöggeler, O. "Metaphysik und Seinstopik bei Heidegger." *Philosophisches Jahrbuch* 70 (1962-63):118-37. Translated by P. Emad as "Metaphysics and Topology of Being in Heidegger." *Man and World* 8 (1975):3-27.

———. *Der Denkweg Martin Heideggers*. Pfullingen: Neske, 1963; second augmented edition, 1983.

———. "'Historicity' in Heidegger's Late Work." *The Southwestern Journal of Philosophy* 4, no. 3 (1973):53-73.

———. "Heideggers Begegnung mit Hölderlin." *Man and World* 10, no. 1 (1977): 569-86.

———. "Wovor die Angst sich ängstet." *Zeitwende* 51 (1980):1-18.

———' "Heidegger und die hermeneutische Theologie." *Verifikationen: Festschrift für Gerhard Ebeling zum 70. Geburtstag*. Hrsg. E. Jungel, J. Wallmann, and W. Werbek, pp. 475-98. Tübingen: J. C. B. Mohr, 1982.

———. "Neue Wege mit Heidegger?" *Philosophische Rundschau* 29 (1982):39-71.

———. "Temporal Interpretation and Hermeneutic Philosophy." In *Phenomenology: Dialogues and Bridges*, edited by R. Bruzina and B. Wilshire, pp. 79-97. Albany, N.Y.: SUNY Press, 1982.

Pugliese, O. *Vermittlung und Kehre*. Freiburg: Alber, 1965.

Renaut, A. "La fin de Heidegger et la tâche de la philosophie." *Les Études Philosophiques*, no. 4 (1977), pp. 485-92.

Richardson, W. "Heidegger and the Origin of Language." *International Philosophical Quarterly* 2 (1962):404-16.

———. *Heidegger: Through Phenomenology to Thought*. The Hague: Nijhoff, 1963.

Sachsse, H. "Was ist Metaphysik?" *Zeitschrift für Philosophische Forschung* 28 (1974):67-93.

Sallis, J. "Toward the Showing of Language." *Southwestern Journal of Philosophy* 4 (1973):75-83.

Sallis, J., ed. *Heidegger and the path of thinking*. Pittsburgh: Duquesne Univ. Press, 1970.

———. *Radical Phenomenology*. Atlantic Highlands, N.J.: Humanities Press, 1978.

Sallis, J., and Maly, K., eds. *Heraclitean Fragments*. University, Ala.: Univ. of Alabama Press, 1980.

Schlüter, J. *Heidegger und Parmenides*. Bonn: Bouvier, 1979.

Schöfer, E. *Die Sprache Heideggers.* Pfulligen: Neske, 1962.

Schürmann, R. "Political Thinking in Heidegger." *Social Research* 45, no. 1 (1978):191-221.

——. "The Ontological Difference and political Philosophy." *Philosophy and Phenomenological Research* 40 (1979):99-122.

——. *La principe d'anarchie.* Paris: Seuil, 1982.

——. "On Self-Regulation and Transgression." *Social Research* 49, no. 4 (1982): 1029-46.

Schulz, W. *Philosophie in der veränderten Welt.* Pfullingen: Neske, 1972.

Sheehan, T. "Heidegger, Aristotle and Phenomenology." *Philosophy Today* 19 (1975):87-94.

——. "Heidegger's 'Introduction to the Phenomenology of Religion,' 1920-21." *The Personalist*, 1979, pp. 312-24.

——. "The 'Original Form' of 'Sein und Zeit': Heidegger's 'Der Begriff der Zeit.'" *The Journal of the British Society of Phenomenology* 10, no. 2 (1979):78-83.

——. "Heidegger's Topic: Excess, Recess, Access." *Tijdschrift voor Filosofie* 41 (1979):615-35.

——. "Heidegger's Philosophy of Mind." *Contemporary Philosophy* vol. 4, pp. 287-318. The Hague: Nijhoff, 1983.

Sheehan, T., ed. *Heidegger: The Man and the Thinker.* Chicago: Precedent, 1981.

Spanos, W. V., ed. *Martin Heidegger and the Question of Literature.* Bloomington, Ind.: Indiana Univ. Press, 1976.

Stambaugh, J. "Time and Dialectic in Hegel and Heidegger." *Research in Phenomenology* 4 (1974):87-97.

Taminiaux, J. *Le regard et l'excédent.* The Hague: Nijhoff, 1977.

——. *Recoupements.* Bruxelles: Ousia, 1982.

Welte, B. "God in Heidegger's Thought." Translated by W. J. Kramer in *Philosophy Today* 26 (1982): 85-100.

White, D. A. *Heidegger and the Language of Poetry.* Lincoln, Neb.: Univ. of Nebraska Press, 1978.

Wiplinger, F. *Wahrheit und Geschichtlichkeit.* Freiburg: Alber, 1961.

——. "Ursprüngliche Spracherfahrung und metaphysische Sprachdeutung." *Die Hermeneutische Frage in der Theologie.* Hrsg. O. Loretz and W. Strolz, pp. 21-85. Freiburg: Herder, 1968.

——. *Metaphysik.* Freiburg: Alber, 1976.

Wood, D. "Style and Strategy at the Limits of Philosophy." *The Monist* 63 (1980):494-511.

Wood, D., ed. *Heidegger and Language.* Univ. of Warwick, Coventry: Parousia Press, 1981.

Wood, D., and Bernasconi, R., eds. *Time and Temporality*. Univ. of Warwick, Coventry: Parousia Press, 1982.

Zimmerman, M. *Eclipse of the Self*. Athens, Ohio: Ohio University Press, 1981.

Index

Absence, 43, 83, 84
Absolute knowledge, 2, 10, 82-83
Actuality, 8-9, 83
Adaequatio, 16-17, 66, 83
Aesthetics, 31-37, 45-46. See also
    Overcoming
Agathon, 17, 18, 22
Aletheia (unconcealment), 12, chapter
    2 *passim*, 71, 87, 88
A-letheia, 9, 16, 22-26, 43, 65, 67, 86,
    87
Ambiguity, 11, 39, 44, 78; of
    actuality, 8-9, 83; of *aletheia*,
    21-22, 26; of Being, 4-5, 93; of
    essence, 73; of *Gestell*, 75; of
    language, 94; of *logos*, 60, 62; of
    metaphysics, 25, 57
The Anaximander Fragment, 25, 43,
    46, 86
Andenken (commemorative thinking),
    11, 53, 61, 87
Aneignung, 13, 16, 17, 88, 92
Angst. See Anxiety
Another Beginning, 11, 12, 45, 63, 66,
    85, 88, 89, 90, 92, 96 n15
Anspruch, 54, 59, 71-72
Anxiety, 54-60, 72, 84, 94
Appropriation. See *Aneignung;*
    Ereignis
Aquinas, Saint Thomas, 18, 26, 66
Aristotle, 2, 4, 16, 43, 49, 55, 71

Art, death of, 36-37. See also
    Aesthetics
Assertion, 16, 19-21, 66, 76, 77, 93
Aufhebung, 3, 15
Avicenna, 16

Basic Problems of Phenomenology, 2,
    12
Bauch, Kurt, 31
Beautiful, 22, 32, 33, 51
Beginning, 5-6, 10, 12, 18, 87, 88. See
    also Another Beginning
Begriff, 76-77
Being, 2, 4-5, 57, 86-87, 93. See also
    Oblivion of Being; Truth of Being;
    Words for Being
Being and Time, 4, 15-17, 18, 21, 30,
    40, 43, 49, 69-70, 81, 88, 93
Bildung, 10
Böhlendorff, Casimir Ulrich, 92
Boredom, 72-73
Bringing forth. See *Poiesis*

Carnap, Rudolf, 88
Certainty, 3, 15, 68
Claim. See *Anspruch*
Clearing. See *Lichtung*
Commemorative Thinking. See
    Andenken
Completion. See *Vollendung*
Concealment, 4, 15, 16, 67-69, 87

Concept. See *Begriff*
Correctness, 17, 19-23, 66-67
Correspondence Theory of Truth. See
    Adaequatio and *Homoiosis*

Danger. See *Gefahr*
Dasein, 16, 35, 37, 55-56, 72, 76-77
Default. See God, default of
Descartes, René, 3, 18, 49, 68
Destiny, 9, 30, 34, 35, 41, 56, 75, 81
Destruction, 4, 17, 43, 88
Dialectic, 3, 7, 8, 9, 78, 82
Dialogue, 83, 91; between thinkers,
    3-4, 6, 9, 12; with poets 29-31,
    42, 46, 52-53
Discordance, 22, 33, 35
Double reading, 12, 23, 34, 54, 58-59,
    64, 93
Dread *(Entsetzen)*, 33, 35

Education. See *Bildung*
Eliot, T. S., 30, 95
End of Philosophy, 2, 4-7, 11-12, 37,
    45, 56, 61-62, 65, 68. See also
    Vollendung
*The End of Philosophy and the Task
    of Thinking*, 18-19, 20, 23-24
Epoch, 7-8, 35, 40, 43, 95
Ereignis, 85-95
Erinnerung, 9-11, 18, 25-26, 41, 45,
    56-57, 69, 83, 84-85
Errancy, 8, 9, 67
Essence. See *Wesen*
Establish. See *Stiftung*
Excess, 8, 38, 44
Experience, in George, 51, 53; in
    Heidegger and Hegel, 1, 4-5, 12,
    81-85; in Hölderlin, 90; natural,
    23; primordial, 43, 88; of anxiety,
    54-55, 57, 58; of oblivion of
    Being, 45, 59; of technology, 10,
    86

Ficino, Marsilio, 33
Formation. See *Bildung*
Friedländer, Paul, 19-21
Fulfillment. See *Vollendung*

Gadamer, Hans-Georg, 1-2, 4, 22, 32
Gathering, 6-7, 9, 15, 49, 61-62
Gefahr, 74-75, 86
Gelassenheit, 66-67, 89
Geläut der Stille, 59, 62-63, 77, 87,
    95
George, Stefan, 31, 49-53, 58-63, 65,
    67, 70, 77, 81, 84, 87, 89, 91, 93
Gestell, 71, 73-75
God/Gods, 37, 39, 42-43, 60-61, 66;
    death of, 11, 35; default of, 35,
    41-42, 84, 90
Goethe, Johann Wolfgang von, 30
Good. See *Agathon*

Hegel G. W. F., chapter one *passim*,
    36-37, 69, 81-85, 90
  Works: *Lectures on the History of
    Philosophy*, 2, 11; *Phenomenology
    of Spirit*, 2, 7, 10, 15, 76-78, 82;
    Science of Logic, 3
Hegel and the Greeks, 15, 20
Hegel's Concept of Experience, 82-8
Heraclitus, 36, 45
Hesiod, 19
Hölderlin, Friedrich, Heidegger's
    dialogue with, 25, 35, 43, 49, 52,
    59, 90-92. Poems: *Am Quell der
    Donau*, 39; *Andenken*, 38; *Brot
    und Wein*, 41, 60-61; *Heimkunft*,
    42; *Friedensfeier*, 91; *Patmos*, 74,
    86; *Wie wenn am Feiertage*, 31,
    38-42, 44-45, 60, 62
Hölderlin and the Essence of Poetry,
    31, 37-38, 46
Holy, 31, 38-42, 60-61, 84, 90-91
Homer, 20

Homoiosis, 17, 22
Husserl, Edmund, 82
Hymn, 40, 42, 62, 91

Identity and Difference, 15
Ideas, Platonic, 17, 18, 22, 75
Institute. See *Stiftung*

Janus head, 11, 75

Kant, Immanuel, 3, 6-7, 13, 31, 33,
    66
Kehre. See Turning

Language, instrumentalist theory of,
    51, 91; originary character of, 37,
    51, 52; study of, 65; of
    metaphysics, 57, 69-70, 92, 94.
    See also *logos*
Law, 39, 60-61
Letter on Humanism, 42, 69-70, 73,
    90
Lichtung (clearing), 16, 19, 22, 23, 55.
    See also Open
Logos, 24, 58, 60-63, 70, 77, 86, 87

Messkirch's Seventh Centennial, 72-74
Merleau-Ponty, Maurice, 30-31, 39, 42
Metaphysics, 55; leave to itself, 89;
    unity of, 7, 9-11, 46, 70, 87. See
    also Overcoming; Language
Metaphysics as History of Being, 8

Nameless, 92, 94
Names, 40, 60. See also Words for
    Being
Nature, 38-39, 42, 45, 71
Neo-Kantian, 35
Nietzsche, Friedrich, 11, 18, 33-35,
    91
Nietzsche, 31-36, 95
Nomos, 60

Non-essence, 94
Non-metaphysical, 92
Not-yet metaphysical, 24, 27
Nothing, 54-56, 58, 60, 83

Objectification, 93
Oblivion of Being, 25, 57, 74, 85-87;
    as aesthetics, 34; as inversion of
    Hegel, 2, 5, 6-8; as technology, 72;
    underlying *Being and Time*, 49,
    70, 81
On the Essence of Truth, 16-17,
    65-70
On the Way to Language, 49, 51-53,
    58-63, 65, 91
Ontological Difference, 15, 39, 56, 89
Open, 39, 42, 55
Openness, 66-68
Origin, 36-37, 39-40, 59
Orthotes. See Correctness
The Origin of the Work of Art, 31,
    35-37, 39, 40, 44, 51
Overcoming, 4, 11, 34, 38; of
    aesthetics, 31-32, 34, 36, 38, 40,
    45, 55-57; of metaphysics, 66, 67,
    87-89. See also *Verwindung*

Parmenides, 5-7, 12, 16, 23-26
Parousia, 83, 85
Perfection. See *Vollkommenheit*
Phenomenology, 15-16, 43, 62, 65,
    70, 73, 83, 85, 93
Physis, 45, 71
Pindar, 29, 39
Plato, 4, 17-26, 31, 33, 43, 71, 93.
    See also Ideas, Platonic
Plato's Doctrine of Truth, 17-19,
    22-23
Platonism, 33, 34
Poiesis, 37, 71, 73-75, 77
Presence, 25, 60, 62, 71, 83. See also
    Absence

Progress, 8, 10, 11
Project, 16, 30, 40, 52
Provisionality, 44, 92–93

The Question concerning Technology,
    37, 70–75, 85, 86

Rapture, 33, 36
Reason, 7, 67, 77
Recollection. See *Erinnerung*
Releasement. See *Gelassenheit*
Remembrance. See *Erinnerung*
Renunciation, 50, 51, 53, 55, 58–59,
    62, 77, 87, 93, 94
Rereading. See Double Reading
Retrogression, 11, 16. See also Step
    Back
Rettung, 74–75, 86
Rilke, Rainer Maria, 41
Rupture, 12, 36

Saving power. See *Rettung*
Saying not-saying, 77–78, 85, 87, 91,
    93–95
Saying of a turning, 66, 75, 76–78. See
    also Turning
Schopenhauer, Arthur, 33
Semele, 41, 45
Sequence, 8, 11–12, 57
Silence, 54–63, 74, 91–95; of the poet,
    40, 42, 52–53. See also *Geläut
    der Stille*; Saying not-saying
Simmel, Georg, 81–82
Song, 50, 91
Sophocles, 60, 61, 63
Speculative Proposition, 3, 6, 76–78
Sprache, 63
Step Back, 15, 25. See also
    Retrogression
Stiftung, 38, 44, 46, 51
Sublation. See *Aufhebung*

Technology, 5, 10, 70–75, 78, 84, 85,
    86, 91–92
Time and Being, 8, 89, 95
Trace, 25, 42, 43, 46, 62, 68, 87, 88,
    94
Trakl, Georg, 59
Transcendentals, 16, 66, 67
Transformation, 51; of man, 56, 82,
    91; of language, 57, 59–60, 62, 66,
    87, 91–92, 94; of thinking, 67, 85,
    92; of the essence of truth, 68, 83;
    of essence, 70, 73, 75; of Being
    into Ereignis, 87
Transitions, 8, 9, 17, 18, 21, 83
Truth, 12, 15, 17–23, 32, 33; changes
    in essence of, 37, 65–70, 94
Truth of Being, 4, 70, 73, 87, 90
Turning, 67, 69, 73, 74, 85, 93. See
    also Saying of a turning

Überfluss. See Excess
Unconcealment, 4, 16, 22. See also
    Aletheia
Unsaid, 4, 5, 17, 85
Unsayable, 52, 53

Van Gogh, Vincent, 31, 36, 84
Versammlung. See Gathering
Verwindung, 88–89
Volkmann-Schluck, Karl-Heinz, 53
Vollendung, 6, 9, 18, 57, 77, 88, 91
Vollkommenheit, 6, 11

Wesen, 65–70, 73–75, 77–78, 84, 94
What is Metaphysics? 54–56, 58, 70,
    72–73, 93; Introduction to, 25, 54,
    56, 58; Postscript to, 25, 31,
    54–56, 58
Words for Being, 11, 39–40, 43–44,
    56, 87; lack of, 7, 54, 56–58, 90,
    95
World, 35, 36, 40, 55, 74, 84